The Cheap Way Round

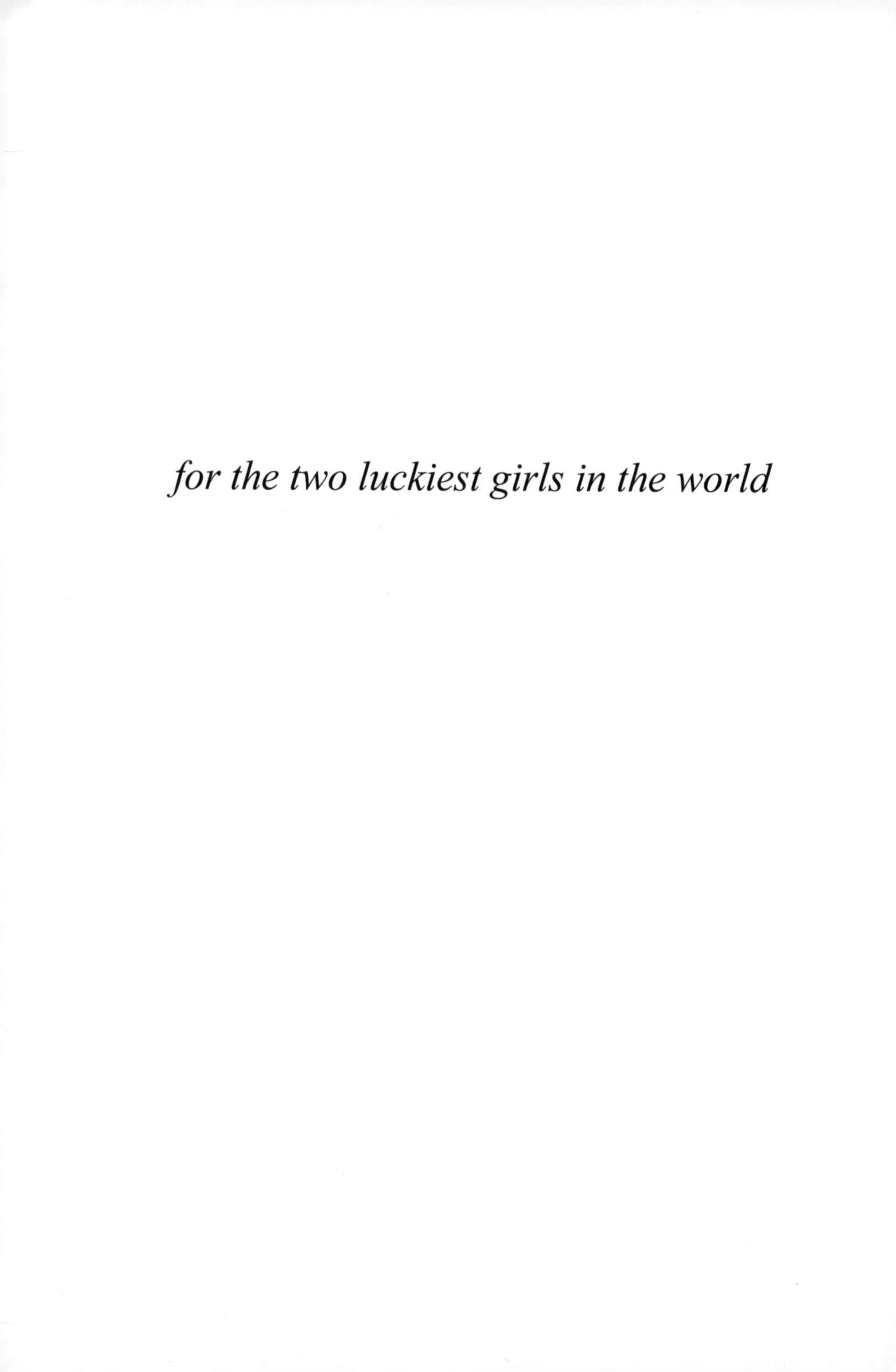

for the two luckiest girls in the world

The Cheap Way Round

Craig Stevenson and John Mackay

Cheapwayround Publishers
East Kilbride

First Published in 2011 by
Cheapwayround Publishers

ISBN No; 978 0 9570252 0 2

Typeset in East Kilbride by
Cheapwayround Publishers

Printed and Bound by
Bell & Bain Ltd., Glasgow

cheapwayround@hotmail.co.uk
www.cheapwayroundpub.co.uk

CONTENTS

Introduction

John; Last summer I turned 60 and to celebrate we had a great party in Vegas.
Unfortunately, I cannot think of much else to fill my time.
My problem is I have no real hobbies. I am hopeless at handy work, I am not much good around the house and have no real interests, till now.
The thing that I have discovered is that the Scottish Parliament is trying to bankrupt the country, I am convinced of this. One of the great things they are doing is giving you a bus pass when you are 60. This lets you go anywhere in Scotland on the bus for nothing. I assume the bus companies are recovering the money from the government, so they must be making a fortune. Most buses are packed with the silver headed.
There are other things you can get for nothing when you reach 60, membership of swimming pools, gyms and other sore things, but travelling on the bus all over Scotland for nothing really took my fancy.
Until I started looking into this mode of transport, I had no idea that there are hundreds of bus routes all over Scotland, and the're all free. The added bonuses are that Scotland is a lovely country, there are pubs or hotels on the route, most buses have toilets (which is essential for over 60s after a few pints) and most importantly, Midges, the wee bastards, can't get at you on the bus, or at least not very much.

I have a friend Stuart, who is secretary of 'The Clyde River Steamer Club', and he spends many of his holidays and weekends travelling around the West of Scotland on the Caledonian Macbraynes Ferries. Unfortunately, the over 60s don't get free travel on the ferries, or trains for that matter (although we get about a third off train fares). As Stuart is a Dentist, he can afford the ferry fares. I think part of my idea to travel about albeit on the cheap, came from him.

I would urge the Scottish parliament to give the over 60s free travel on trains and ferries as well, might as well screw the country as quickly as possible.

By the way, have you ferry travellers ever noticed that all the ferries have the name of the ferries written on them in a foreign language, the wife tells me it's Gaelic, which is our national language. Cal Mac are getting grants every year from the Scottish Parliament, I hope the two Gaelic speakers in Scotland appreciate this.

However, enough of my ranting on about our Parliament wasting money on me and the rest of the over 60s.

When I mentioned my idea to my friend Craig, originally from Auchinleck, he thought it was a good idea, although he would have preferred visiting old mining sites in Ayrshire. Craig is very bad with Arthritis, and although not yet 60, qualifies for a free bus pass. Craig also goes cycling all around the country roads and paths. I have great admiration for him as he is in great pain much of time, especially when listening to my ultra right wing rants after a good few pints of Belhaven Best have been downed.

He has asked me in the past if I fancy cycling around the country. He doesn't ask any more.

So Craig and I have decided to go travelling round Scotland on the Bus, thanks to the Scottish Parliament, bless them.

Although busses are the main mode of transport, we also use Trains and Ferries. We use trains, if possible, for returning from trips, as the availability of toilets is essential, especially after a six pint journey. Some buses do have toilets, but it is a chance we don't like to take, and late on in the day, they can be pretty messy, and if you are not to steady on your legs at this stage of the day, you can emerge from the toilet covered in shit.

We also use ferries, and although you don't get much discount, you get a bit, and makes travelling, especially in the west of Scotland, so much more interesting, and there are bars and toilets on many of the ferries.

The Scottish parliament could do worse than give the over 60s a card to get free, or at least discounted, alcoholic

Craig, and I dressed up for a wedding

beverages, or at least pints. It would also guarantee them election victories for ever. Think of all the over 60s in the country.

Like all great ideas, there are hick-ups. Our wives have mentioned that they would like to join us on some of our trips. I have tried to point out to my wife that as she is still a young thing and as she does not qualify for a bus pass, would have to pay, but she is not put off. She can't understand if most of the travel is free, and we take pieces, how we manage to spent about £50 on a day trip?
Can you imagine the wife on such a trip, 'did you not have a pint in the last place we stopped', all the joy would be taken out of the trip, and we would come home sober, what's that all about.
So Craig and I have been travelling around the country on the cheap. We started locally (we both live in East Kilbride). So the west coast and the Clyde estuary area was our starting point.
Over the next few pages of this, our first attempt at a literary masterpiece, we will attempt to describe in detail, not only where we went, and by what type of transport, but the things that happened on the trips and the people we came in contact with. You will also note that we did walk on occasions, usually because of our lack of ability to read timetables, or when Craig used the web and key'd in our start and end point and believed the crap that is output.
We will also give you our impressions of the bars and hotels we visited, they are only, really vague impressions because most of the trip is usually a blur by the next morning.
Craig did try a video diary of our first trip, but the least said about that the better. Enough to say it was like an episode of Men Behaving Badly-old men.
Before we start. I would like to tell the story of the first day the bus passes started. Seemingly, hundreds of oldies left Glasgow's Buchanan Street Bus Station all morning and

headed for Oban, being about the furthest place you can get to and back in a day and get a walk along the beach, if there is one. It was like the Highland Clearances, only with grey hair and no kilts.

Anyway, as you can imagine, most of them went for the last bus back-hundreds of them. Oban's Bed and Breakfasts did a roaring trade that night.

Craig; *I have always enjoyed travelling. In fact it is true to say that, in my case at least, that the journey is more important than reaching the destination. Not original thought I'll admit. I can't remember who it is that I'm misquoting. It is either an ancient Chinese philosopher or Lee Marvin, but the sentiments are all mine. Anyway, when John came up with the idea of travelling round Scotland on the cheap I was all for it. Taking buses, trains and ferries around the country, stopping in some of my favourite little towns and cities for the odd refreshment and cultural experience is just a marvellous way to spend a few days. Or as it turned out quite a few days.*

It's really quite apt for me to take up travelling around on the buses. That's how I started my working life. Way back in the early 1970s my first job was with Western SMT. I worked in the head office dealing with fare tables and timetables. You would imagine that being a bit of a wiz kid with the timetables would stand me in good stead for my new career as a bus travelling, beer swilling spinner of half remembered stories. I'm afraid too much water has passed under the bridge since that first job. Now I rely on my computer, and of course John, to work out my travel arrangements. I'm not saying it would be impossible for us to plan our travels without using the computer but looking up individual timetables would take a lot of time and effort. Those are two commodities we don't like to squander.

This is what it is all about-a free bus round Scotland

The problem is that neither of us is very competent when it comes to new technology. That would explain why we can both come up with totally different times for the same bus. Or, as in one of our more spectacular slip-ups, the time we managed to invent an entirely new bus route; aka the Tarbet ghost bus. Between ropey planning and the odd refreshment it's a wonder we ever make it back home.

John was much further travelled during his working life than me. Every other week or so he'd be jetting off to somewhere in Europe or America.. To be honest I was always a bit jealous of all this globe-trotting but John is very blasé about it all. He claims it's not much fun when it's work, though he did seem to do a lot of work in Las Vegas. Lucky bugger.

For many years, and he liked to tell everyone about this, frequently, he travelled only in first or business class. I suppose you could say he was hob-knobbing with the elite. People like stressed out, booze raddled media types, MPs on important fact finding trips to endangered rainforests in

the Bahamas or city bankers throwing our cash around like one armed jugglers. It's a different world on the buses.
You meet a different class of traveller on the bus. The passengers tend to be less annoying, predominately older, thanks to John's favourite government initiative, and only a small percentage of them are permanently under the influence of alcohol.
We have had to become quite ruthless when it comes to using the bus. Far too many of the blue rinse brigade have taken up the option of free travel. That means there is no room for chivalry anymore. Survival of the fittest is the name of the game nowadays. One moment of weakness and you could be trapped behind an old biddy wrestling with her Zimmer. It's even worse if they have luggage.
We also take our roles as pub reviewers very seriously. Between the two of us we have about 80 years of beer guzzling experience. So no one is better qualified to rant on about drink and pub culture than we are. And we do, at length.
As we see it every pub has its own character, and usually quite a few strange characters. We like to visit these establishments mid-week and rarely stay late into the night so it tends to be your dedicated bar fly we encounter on our trips.
It is quite amazing how often we meet people who can't wait to share their very personal stories with us. Such is the power of alcohol, or singing ginger as they used to call it down where I come from. Very rarely do these stories have a happy ending. That's another by-product of a life spent abusing booze. But you have to admit I does make for a good day out.
Unlike these upstanding citizens we have to force ourselves to sample the pubs' wares at antisocial hours. It's a

sacrifice, but we are nothing if not diligent. More often than not John has to remind me that what we are doing is bigger than the both of us and we must choke down that extra pint, travel that extra few hundred yards or even put up with a lack of bar stools to get the job done.

I feel it is only fair that if we are going to judge or, more often than not, fabricate the character and culture of the people from those areas we visit, we should also go on record with an insight into our own characters.

My own upbringing was quite tough. I was born and brought up in a 'robust' mining town in Ayrshire. Auchinleck was a hard little place to grow up It's even hard to pronounce.

Back in those days Ayrshire mining towns were places where men were men, and so were quite a few of the women. Almost all of the employment in the area involved coal. Digging it, buying it or stealing it.

There was not what you could call a lot of social mobility in the coal fields. If your father was a miner that was pretty much all you could expect to achieve yourself. The very few who didn't shape up for that career path could expect to find employment above ground, shovelling animal by-products as farm labourers.

There might not have been a lot of chance to better yourself. But there was a sense of community. Legend had it that no one ever needed to lock their doors at night. This was not as you might expect because of the inherent honesty of the common old working chaps but rather because nobody had anything worth stealing.

The pastimes of your average adult male consisted of gambling, binge drinking and smoking heavily. This tended to keep the local population poor, violently antisocial and short lived.

On the plus side this meant there was never a shortage of housing and the town didn't grow too large.

The pubs I remember from my youth were a bit on the rough side. It felt like we were living in a frontier town. The licensing laws didn't help a lot it must be said. At ten minutes to ten everyone would try to buy as much booze as possible then spend the next twenty minutes forcing it down their throats. The festivities would then conclude outside with a series of stimulating debates or, as often as not, a running battle the length of the main street. All in all it wasn't easy growing up there.

Govan on the other hand was worker's paradise. In John's home town the people had it easy. Most of the men were employed in the shipyards where a proficiency at cards was a more valued skill than welding. On the odd days when the workers weren't on strike they tended to spend their time

Bath Night in Govan

pilfering the fixtures and fittings from the ships being kitted out in the yards. John tells me that many homes in the area benefited from this rich source of DIY materials, though it's hard to imagine why anyone would want a ships compass in their living room. Bathroom fixtures were also much favoured items among the good people of Govan and of course there was always a ready supply to be found in the luxury liners being built. The workers would go to great lengths to acquire a large roll top enamel bath. Where else would your upwardly mobile Govanite keep their coal?

It was from this privileged background that John came. I'm not saying that he was born with a silver spoon in his mouth. But at least they had spoons, even if all of their cutlery did have the' Cunard' crest on it.

I believe that our varied backgrounds qualify us to offer our insightful opinions on life, travel and of course beer swilling.

Contained in the following pages is a record of our travels, sometimes humorous, often educational and every now and again true. That is to say, due to the nature of our work there has to be a certain amount of guess work concerning the latter stages of many of our research sessions.

Nae Booze, Nae Bus

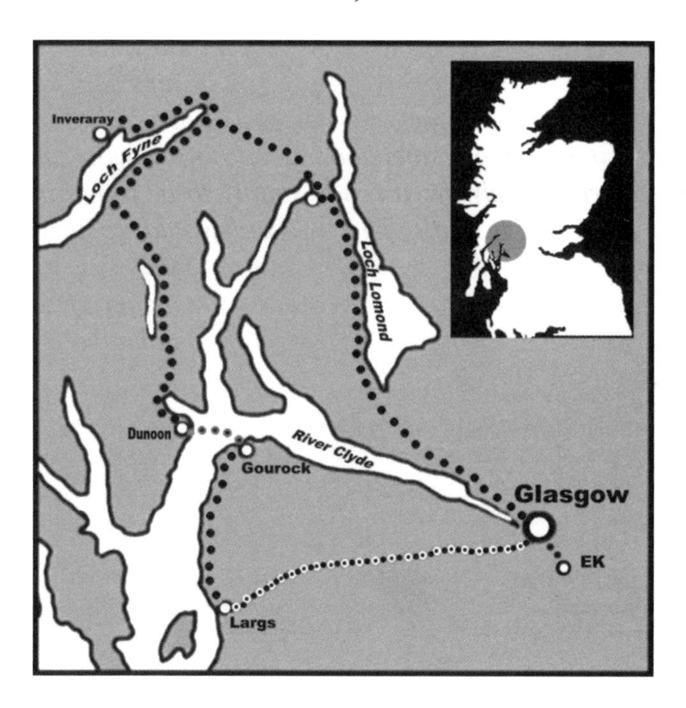

East Kilbride-Glasgow-Tarbet-Arrochar-Inveraray-Dunoon-Gourock-Largs-Glasgow-East Kilbride
(Four Buses, Three Trains-One Ferry-**One Two Mile Walk**)

John; The details above was how it worked out, but it was not as we had planned it, the two mile walk was the choice between spending nearly two hours in Tarbet being eaten alive by midges, or walking to Arrochar. The third, and obvious choice of spending a pleasant one and a half hour (or three pints) in the Bar of the Tarbet Hotel was a non starter as the man in the reception told us the Bar was shut, but we could have a cup of tea. This is at quarter past eleven

for Christ sake, who drinks tea at that, or any time, on a guys day out. We could see the bar. Talk about wonderful Scottish hospitality, it would drive you to drink, or in our case, to walking. Anyway; to start the trip.
After getting the train from East Kilbride to Glasgow, which only costs £0.40p, we had planned to get a Citylink bus from Glasgow direct to Inveraray, and the 10.00am bus seemed to fit the part. It was Craig who, on checking found that I was planning to go to the Invervay Hotel in Tyndrum. Imagine calling a hotel a name like Invervay, I thought it said Inveraray. Tyndrum is obviously trying to get more tourists on the back of idiots like me.
However, on checking the timetables again, and Craig doing his going from here to there trick on the web, we discovered that if we got off at Tarbet, we could get a McGill's bus about ten minutes later. There was of course, no bus, and on checking at the tourist information cabin, were told by the woman that there never has been a McGill's Bus service in this area. What's that all about? Come on McGill's, get a grip.
As the next bus was not for another hour or so, and the Tarbet Hotel was across the road, we thought that as it was 11.15am we could have a couple of pints while we waited.
This bit of Loch Lomond is very touristy, with boat trips and that sort of thing, so we found it hard to believe that the bar was not open. We could have walked into it and helped ourselves. So after trying to explain to the foreign gentleman that the bar should be open, I came up with the idea of walking to Arrochar where I knew there was a hotel and at least one pub. We felt like real hikers walking the two miles to Arrochar. We looked like a couple of bevy merchants.
The Arrochar Hotel looked a bit run down, but there was a man up a ladder who told us the hotel was open. It was like

many medium sized hotels in Scotland, trying to keep the place smart, but with the prices and the midges in the West of Scotland, everyone is going to Spain or Tenerife these days.

The bar was nice with a fabulous view of the loch, although you had to look through the huge mirror behind the bar to see the loch as the seats at the bar faced away from it. However, reversed scenic grandeur is better than none.

We had a couple of pints and the bar maid/receptionist (why can't the Tarbet Hotel do this) was very good-she even got out the timetable for 'West Coast Motor Coaches', for although we were going to catch the Citylink' coach at 1.10pm, she thought the West Coast coach came 10 minutes earlier, at 1.00pm (she was obviously trying to get rid of us). However, when we checked the timetable, we found out that the bus did not run on Monday…it was a Monday.

So we left the hotel at 1.00pm for the short walk to the bus stop, only to see the West Coast bus screaming past.

No beer at the inn

Can nobody get their timetables right? Or maybe we cannot read them properly. It is our first trip after all.

Craig; *Choosing to journey around Scotland by bus seemed like a good idea. The scenery in this country is, in my opinion, the best in the world. However, the planning which went into the first small journey was a bit of an eye opener. Although John was planning the trip it seemed only fair, not to mention safer, for me to check out the route and timetables as well.*

I had decided to let my computer take most of the strain out of the process, and that's where things started to go wrong. Computers are really simple machines and my simple machine is positively moronic. It doesn't work logically. Sometimes it just doesn't work at all. One of the solutions it suggested would have taken 10 hours and that didn't include beer stops.

Somehow, between the two of us, we managed to cobble together a workable timetable.

John's fixation with bladder control tends to shape many of our travel choices. I'm pretty sure he has a spreadsheet presentation showing the mpb (miles per beer) taking into account age and time of day. His eyes light up when he finds out a bus has a toilet on it.

Like John I really appreciate the free travel ticket provided by the Scottish Government, even if I don't particularly like their politics at the moment. That might sound as if I was agreeing with John and I could not let that go unchallenged. Where I believe they should be working to create a more socially inclusive society John is just miffed because they still refuse to bring back capital punishment for dropping litter. Our political differences make for lively debates and, as John wisely points out, we can keep on having the same ones because we never remember how they turn out. This may or may not be due to the fact our debates always seem to take place while propping up a bar.

The first journey, to Inveraray and Dunoon was a bit of a test for me. I really didn't know if I would like this type of day out. Sitting on buses for hours on end might not be as much fun as it sounds.

We reached East Kilbride railway station at about 8.30am for the 8.48am train to Glasgow Central. John was most put out by the fact that the wee man in the ticket office refused to give him the concessionary fare as it was before 9 o'clock. That would have been bad enough but, adding insult to injury, my ticket was accepted. One up for me then.

We arrived at Buchannan Bus Station in good time for our bus to Luss or Tarbet or wherever it was we were supposed to be going. I was never quite sure where we should be getting off the bus. I left it to John to get us there.

Once we arrived in Tarbet we decided that we should at least look like tourists and so we went down to stare at Loch Lomond for 5 minutes. That done it was back to the real business of the day; the buying and consumption of beer. We then encountered our first major setback of the day, the Tarbet Hotel bar was closed.

At least the guy in the hotel foyer apologised. He was obviously foreign and hadn't been in the country for long. If he stays here long enough he will learn that Scottish workers in the service industry never ever apologise, are traditionally surly, unhelpful and patronising. The standard response should have been to look at us as if we had just arrived by muck spreader, shrug his shoulders and return to checking his phone for text messages. There was nothing left for us but to wait for the bus. It turns out we had more chance of a drink in the hotel than catch the bus. There was no bus and

according to the Tourist Information Office there never has been one.
Half an hour later and a sweaty trek through a midge infested forest we arrived at the civilised little hamlet of Arrochar. Civilised in that it had a bar and it was open. Two pints of good humour later and we were ready to journey on.
John; The Citylink coach arrived on time and took us over The Rest and be Thankful and round the top of Loch Fyne to Inveraray. It is a beautiful run through wonderful countryside that cannot be beaten anywhere, and there was a toilet on the bus.
When the bus got close to Inveraray, we noticed a massive cruiser in the bay. It was worth millions, and when we got off the bus, we saw that the front of the town had been transformed into a massive film set, they must have spent thousands doing all the work. However, as we had only 15 minutes here because of earlier timetable screw ups, we had to find out quickly what was happening and meet Brad Pitt or whoever was in the film to make the wife jealous.
I spoke to a wee man in costume having a smoke, obviously an extra, who told me they were making a film about the making of Harris Tweed. What a downer, and why are they making it in Inveraray, and who gives a shit?
We did not have any time to visit the scenic grandeur of Inveraray or its castle, not that we had any intention of ever doing it, but we did manage a rushed drink in the hotel across from the bus stop-scenic grandeur no more.
So without time to visit the castle or the famous Inveraray Inn we got on our next bus to Dunoon.
I don't think there is an Inveraray Inn, but there is a great song which starts- *'It's a rare wee inn, the Inveraray Inn'*
Craig; *Our next bus would take us to Inveraray and as you would expect it was full of 'blue rinsers'. The driver*

announced that when he had left Inveraray that morning there had been snow on the ground. There were some audible gasps from the 'rinsers' at this news, which meant either they were very surprised or something had gone wrong with their medication. He explained that a film crew were working in the town and had painted the roofs and harbour area to look wintry. John was suddenly interested. Fame beckoned. He was devastated to find it was just a documentary being made.
It was interesting to see how they had transformed the harbour area into a winter scene in the 1800s.
We only had 15 minutes before our next bus and John was worried about the lack of a toilet on it so we had to visit a hotel to use its facilities. It seemed to me that it would be really unfair to be spending a penny in the hotel without spending a few pounds as well. I settled for a half pint of lager. John not to be out done ordered a small bottle of red wine.
Once we were on the road again we had our sandwiches. I washed mine down with a can of juice while John furtively swigged away at his wine. I suggested that for a touch of authenticity he should have asked for a small brown paper bag with it.
John; The 'West Coast' bus left on time (no toilet), and after re-tracing the previous buses route for five minutes or so, took a right turn, and headed down the other side of Loch Fyne to Strachur.
An interesting fact (I think) about this stretch of road is that it was built by Italian prisoners of war. It is a great road and fairly straight, I suppose so the Italians could run backwards without falling off into the ditches.
During this section of the journey we had our pieces. I had corn beef with English mustard on plain bread. You canny

'Lights, cameras and no action'

beat corned beef and it doesn't't make the bread soggy. Craig had something else.

An interesting thing about Craig is that he won't eat Corned Beef because it's from the Argentine, and we were at war with them. What I can't understand is that, like all people of mining stock, he hates Margaret Thatcher. I'd have thought he would be a fan of Corned Beef. Come to think of it, if we didn't eat food from places we have been at war with, we would all starve. Anyway, to continue.

At Strachur we took a left and headed to Dunoon. I have never been on this road before and it is really nice with great views.

Craig; *Dunoon was our next refreshment stop.*

'The View' was quite a sight. From the outside this bar looked more like a small factory or industrial unit. Inside it had everything a couple of weary travellers could wish for;

draught beer and toilets. Actually it had much more than that. Comfy seats and a spectacular view of the Clyde estuary would be reason enough to spend some time in The View. We sat at the large windows watching our boat crossing over from Gourock. By this time the weather had really improved with hardly a cloud in the sky.

John; About one hour after leaving Inveraray, we got to Dunoon. I have only been to Dunoon once many years ago and as the bus drove through the town on the way to the pier, where this part of the journey ended, I was glad of the absence. Having said that, it was a glorious day, the scenery was lovely and we told our wives we spent the 40 minutes admiring the view. The View is the bar opposite the pier, and what a great view it is. The beer was not too bad either.

We got on the Cal Mac ferry 'Saturn'. Of course the name is also in Gaelic. I forgot to write down the Gaelic name,

Can juggling on the way back to Gourock

or, maybe I had no intention of ever doing it. We had a lovely sail over to Gourock. We sat outside and enjoyed the fabulous scenery and a can of lager, no draught on the ferries, although there is a toilet..

Craig; *Upstairs on the ferry we sat back to enjoy the trip and of course a couple of cold beers.*

The bar we chose to visit in Largs had very definitely seen better days as had most of its customers. A couple of beers later and the place began to look much inviting. Unfortunately the customers were still pretty sore on the eye.

As we had been travelling around the Clyde Estuary I had been trying to make a video diary of the day. When we arrived at Largs railway station John decided that he would like to have a go at filming. That is the reason why the video diary contains a three minute segment showing an index finger blocking half the screen. To be honest if that had been the worst thing on the video I would be a happy man. It is unlikely that it will ever see the light of day. Perhaps it would be a good idea if the camera manufacturers put a warning label on every box: DO NOT OPERATE CAMERA WHEN EVEN SLIGHTLY TIPSY.

John; At Gourock we waited 10 minutes and, would you believe it, a McGill's bus turned up to take us to Largs, our next destination. So there's one of them at least.

It's a lovely journey by bus from Gourock to Largs. You pass the Cloch Lighthouse, go through the small village of Inverkip, which you bypass if you drive, past Weymss Bay, where the ferry leaves for Rothesay, my favourite place in Scotland, and along the edge of the Clyde estuary, with great views of Bute, to Largs. We got little peace on the bus as there were four Jakies on the bus who were pissed and drug addicts. You can always tell them by the way they cannot stop talking, and they all talk loudly through their noses, or what's left of them. They got off at Wemyss Bay, to get the ferry to Rothesay, or a top up in some local pub.

We got off the bus at Largs, and after a cursory look at the view over to the Great Cumbrae, headed into the nearest bar where we had a couple of pints. A side note at this stage is that Craig drinks lager, Tennents if available, and I drink 70 Shilling, Velvet or Best (in the old days it was just a pint of Heavy). We could relax drinking in the knowledge that the next journey was by train, with a toilet.

We then bought a Fish Supper which we ate sitting on the front at Largs, watching the ferry, with the Gaelic name, sail over to Millport. Craig's wife, Irene by the way, loves Millport, (including Craig, that's two pretty run down things she loves). We then walked up the main street and got the train to Glasgow. The train runs along the coast with great views over to Arran and passes lovely villages, but then heads for places like Kilwinning, Johnson and Paisley. You don't want to get thrown off the train in any of these.

And so, an hour later we arrived in Glasgow Central Station, in my opinion one of the nicest in Britain. Most sober people would then walk to the platform for the East Kilbride train and get on, but not the traveller who knows the 'Horse Shoe Bar' is only a two minute walk away.

The Horse Shoe is without doubt Glasgow's best pub, and one of the last ones you can walk into and hear yourself ask for a pint. The drink, service and pies are all great and there is never any hassle. So we had a couple of pints before getting back to the Central Station and the train to East Kilbride. It is a 20 minute walk home through the old village, so we obviously stopped for a couple of pints in the Monty (Montgomery Arms). This is one of the best pubs in East Kilbride, it won *the Daily Record*, or was it t*he Evening Times* Pub of the year a few years ago.

The Monty, our base camp (never seen us sober)

Craig; *As planned we arrived back in Glasgow in time for a couple of beers in the Horse Shoe Bar, good beer at a decent price. We decided to film another entry in the video diary while standing at the bar. In any other place this would have attracted at least a little attention, not here. I would imagine that if you were a regular in the Horse Shoe you've pretty much seen it all before. Our last port of call 'The Monty' was reached at about 9 o'clock after a quick journey up from Glasgow. Once again a couple of drinks were required, this time to mark the end of a great day out. As far as I'm concerned the journey from the pub back to my house might as well have been made by helicopter as I have no recollection of it. Fatigue must have been setting in!*

A couple of days after our epic trek I met John to discuss the whole thing. I told him he had made a good job of summing up the journey on video while we were sitting in the Monty. I said it was wasted a little bit near the end when that drunk tried to get in on the act. " Did you recognise him?" John asked. " Yes, that would be me " I replied.

John; All that was left was the short walk home, and although both our wives were in bed sleeping, they knew we were pretty drunk. Kate (my wife) even knew how many pints I had, that's amazing as I had no idea.

And that was the end of our first cheap way round trip in Scotland.

You will notice in the list of spends that the fish supper cost £5.00, sometimes you can pay much more than that. When I was a lad, fish suppers were fairly cheap, but sometimes if you had lots of money you could afford a chicken supper.

.Nowadays, a chicken supper is a good bit cheaper than a fish supper. Shows how things have changed.

Craig; *Just shows how old you are John.*

Our spends for the day;

Bus fares;	zero
Train fares	£4.00
Ferry fares	£3.00
Food	£5.00 (fish supper)
Drink	£27.00 (essential)
Total	**£39.00**

Never ask a Local

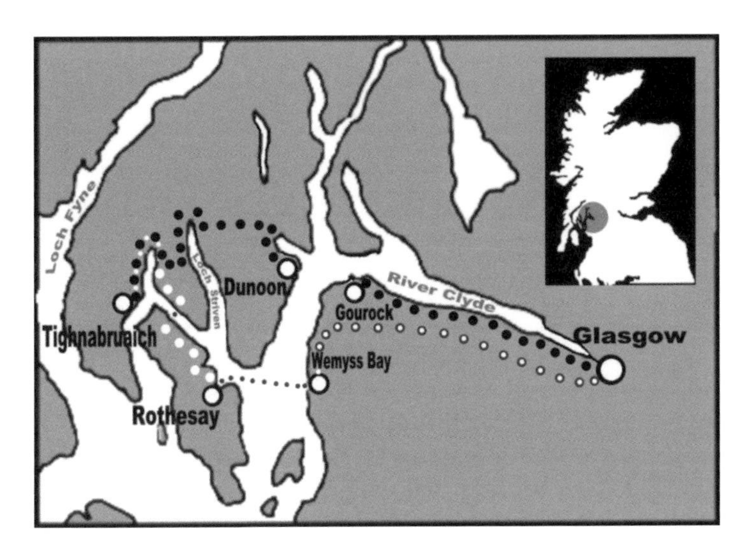

East Kilbride-Glasgow-Gourock-Dunoon-Tighnabruaich-Rothesay-Wemyss Bay-Glasgow-East Kilbride
five buses-three trains-three ferries

John; In the spirit of eaksy peaksy, I allowed Craig to arrange this trip, and although some of the place names above are the same as our first trip, the vast majority of the trip was different, although I have nothing against going to the same places more than once if they are worth it, and the pubs good.
As this was our second journey and as we had the idea of keeping some kind or journal, we have included more detailed times of the transport and road numbers, if possible. Remembering of course that the main reason for the trips is the scenery and a few pints.

Destination Tighnabruaich

The first, and usual part of the journey was the £0.40p single train journey into Glasgow Central. The train left East Kilbride at 9.48 am and arrived at 10.18am, well that's what it said on the timetable, and we seemed to arrive on time.
We then walked up to St. Vincent Street to get the McGill's bus number 901 at 10.31am. Remembering it was McGill's that failed to turn up on our first trip, Craig felt we should give them another chance, plus it was the only bus that went direct from Glasgow to Gourock. The bus went from Glasgow to Largs via Gourock. At 10.30am a Citylink bus number 901 with Largs marked as its destination came along and we waved it down in a panic. The driver said that they turned off before Gourock. He said we could get on his bus, get off before Gourock and get another local bus to Gourock. We decided, with unbelievable faith to wait for the McGill's bus with the same number. Again, what's that all about, are there not plenty of numbers to pick from?
Amazingly, and only 10 minutes late, the McGill's bus turned up. We got on, didn't pay our fare and the bus fairly belted along the M8 from Glasgow to Greenock where it

stopped at the local bus station for about 10 minutes, I suppose to ensure that the 10 minutes he had made up by nearly shaking us to death on the M8 (remember, all the people on the bus were over 60) would be lost again.

Craig; *This journey was my first and possibly last attempt at solo planning. It's not that it didn't workout, in fact it was more or less perfect, it was just too nerve wracking. Being a bit of a pessimist at the best of times doesn't help. I was constantly on edge, waiting for something catastrophic to happen. There were sleepless nights worrying about bus timetables and connections. Worse than that when I did get some sleep I was plagued by nightmares. They generally took the form of me running after a McGill's bus, whose driver could neither hear or see me frantically banging on the door.*

At last the morning of our journey arrived. I was packed and ready, mainly because of the sleepless night I'd just endured. For once I had remembered to pack my umbrella. Most people would think that I had done this in case it might rain. Not so. I have found that, without exception, every time I take a brolly out with me not one drop of rain will fall wherever I travel. This simplifies things for me as I don't have to rely on the weather forecast on the telly. I suppose I could make a little money hiring myself out to local fetes and sporting events guaranteeing good weather for that day. The 'experts' who do actually get paid to predict weather conditions are not exactly reliable. When you think of how much money the BBC must spend on their weather forecasts, only to make an arse of it, a person, not unlike John, could get very angry.

The journey began at East Kilbride railway station. This time round we both got the concessionary fare as I had planned the trip to start after 9 0'clock, mainly because I couldn't stand to see the disappointment on John's face if he had failed yet again at the first hurdle. The journey down to Glasgow was uneventful, but waiting for our connecting bus was a bit more traumatic. It was a McGill's bus after all. Just to heighten the drama of the occasion it was late. As we got on board I averted my eyes just in case the driver looked like the one in my nightmare. A few minutes later we were hurtling along at a terrific speed. That's terrific in the terrifying sense of the word. I didn't know those buses could move so fast. Every now and then I glanced out the back window to see if someone was chasing us.

When we got to Greenock we realised why the driver had been piling on the speed. Waiting for the bus was a very large crowd of passengers. They were in all shapes and sizes but, they had one thing in common. The were in no hurry to get on the bus. I don't know if it was a physical thing or if they were all just a bit thick but since the driver obviously knew what to expect here they must do this on a regular basis. Maybe they should run night classes in Greenock teaching the good folk of the town simple techniques in entering and exiting public transport. Why the whole town would be afflicted is anyone's guess, but I made a mental note to avoid drinking the tap water if I ever find myself down that way again, just in case.

Anyway we lost all the time our driver had saved with his cannonball run through the West of Scotland. That was time we could have put to good use soaking up some scenic grandeur and, or, having an extra pint. It must be said that our driver did his level best to make up this time by once again driving like a loony, but even he had to stop at some of the red lights.

The pub we decided to visit while we waited for the ferry to Dunoon was what I would call West Coast Traditional. That is to say, it was a dump. A very nice wee dump all the same. It wasn't exactly dirty, just well used.. During the bad old days, pre- smoking ban, it would have benefited from a good smoke screen covering up all its cracks and scrapes. Nowadays, thanks to our caring Scottish Parliament, we get to see our pubs, warts and all, not to mention savour all those little aromas which went unnoticed in the old foggy days. At that time of day pubs like this are frequented by a certain type of drinker. The main groups would be, the work shy, the retired and of course the intrepid explorers, such as ourselves. After a very reasonable pint we made our way to the ferry terminal.

John; We got off the bus only one stop early (my fault) at about 11.30am and walked along the front at Gourock and into a pub as we had time for a pint before we headed to the ferry to Dunoon. We had time because we planned it that way-got to get the priorities right.

What you would call old men's pubs in Scottish towns are all the same at about opening time in the morning, especially Mondays (this was a Monday). There are usually about six people in who look as if they have slept in their clothes and they are always reading the Racing Post. Craig and I fitted in no problem.

After one pint we headed down to the ticket office. Craig had cleverly worked out that the three ferries we were planning to go on today were included in a special ticket called an 'Island Hopscotch', the idea is that instead of buying three tickets at a total cost of £8.50, we only paid £7.90.

We asked if oldies got a discount and the ticket lady just laughed. We took that as a no. We bought the tickets anyway even though the saving was pretty poor. If Calmac can afford to put Gaelic writing on every ferry, surely they can give over 60s' a decent discount.

We got on the ferry from Gourock to Dunoon, which is the opposite way from our first trip. The ferry left at about 12.40pm. We had a lovely sail and ate some of our pieces on the ferry. I had corned beef again, I love it. Craig still hates the Argies.

We were lucky again with the weather which was glorious.

We arrived in Dunoon at the back of one (detailed times are starting to go out the window). As our bus to Tighnabruaich was not leaving till about two something, we spent the time admiring the view, the View being the pub we were in during our first trip. The barmaid said hello to us when we went in. We're beginning to feel like locals.

Craig; *On the ferry we decided that it was time to eat our sandwiches. John had been desperate to get into them since we got on the train in East Kilbride.*

In Dunoon we once again took in the View, if you know what I mean.

The best I could say about the next part of the journey would be that it was an experience. An experience I have no wish to repeat. I've had physiotherapists mangle my spine and it was less painful than the bus run from Dunoon to Tighnabruaich My vertebrae stood up to the pummelling it received, but I suspect there will be complications later in life.

It was quite funny when our little torture machine finally stopped at a lay-bye and we had to change buses. No one had actually told us that this would happen but it seemed quite natural. Our new bus was driven by a chap called Donald, so one of the passengers told us. Travelling along the remainder of the road to Tighnabruaich Donald took a more leisurely approach to driving, very smooth indeed. It occurred to me that our new bus was in much better condition than the last one. The reason for this was obvious, to me at least.

New buses would be put on the tamer part of the route where they would stay until they showed signs of wear. They would then be switched to the roller coaster run to end their days. I would imagine there's a similar story when it comes to allocating drivers to the routes. The only difference being the newer drivers would be sent out in the older buses. Only a select few could have the nerve to endure the first leg of the Tighnabruaich run.

I expect Donald was invalided out of that route, probably after a nervous breakdown. Now he spends his working day ferrying school children and drunks up and down the A 8003. Though how anyone can describe this meandering track as an A road is beyond me.

Apart from chatting to a local who had absolutely no local knowledge whatsoever the rest of the journey to Tighnabruaich was fairly uneventful. I did manage to catch a glimpse of the view at the top of the hill just before Tighnabruaich, looking down the Kyles of Bute. The last time I saw it I was on one of my cycling tours and the view so impressed me I forgot how tired I was. This time there was little chance to take in the scenery as it was a very steep incline with many tricky turns and I was a little concerned that Donald might not be up to the task. His nerve held and he let us off at the front door of the Royal Hotel.

John; A very small bus left on time and headed up the B836, which is a single track road full of corners and bumps. I felt sorry for Craig as he felt every bump. He is convinced he got off the bus two inches shorter. Amazingly, and to our surprise, the bus stopped in the middle of nowhere and there was another bus waiting to pick us up for the rest of the journey. I don't know why. This was a bigger bus with springs and everything, except a toilet. However, as we came near our destination Tighnabruaich, we passed what is easily

the best view in Scotland, if not the world. Before you reach Tighnabruaich, you climb up a huge hill and look down on the Kyles of Bute, at the narrows. It is absolutely stunning, especially on a good day.
Like Craig, there are many people of a mature age who suffer from arthritis and may have problems turning their head to see a great view which may pass quickly. I have an idea that could solve this. There should be several window seats on each bus that can swivel, like a computer chair, so that if a person cannot turn his or her head independently, all they need to do is spin the chair round and they would see the lovely scenery passing by as easily as the bendy people. The only problem I can see is that on roads with a lot of sudden corners, some oldies may come shooting off their seats, unless they were wearing seat belts. Mind you, if they were wearing seat belts, they might well come off the bus in the same state as you did when you came off the Waltzer at the carnival when you were young. Anyway, back to the trip. We had a commentary on the area from a man sitting in front of us. When he heard me trying to say I had not been in this area for a while, he assumed I had never been here and bored us to death with facts, we already knew, for over ten minutes.
We didn't want to interrupt him as he seemed to be enjoying himself, and he was English.
As we were still unsure of our ability to read, or believe the timetables, especially in the area we were in, where, apart from the usual complications you get on timetables, this areas timetables varies between schooldays and holidays. We asked the English travel guide we had picked up if there was a bus, about an hour after we arrived, that would take us to Rothesay, on the Isle of Bute. He assured us that there was no such bus, 'and I've lived here for ten years'. Thankfully,

A wee bit of scenic grandeur

the wee woman in front of him, who had heard every word, as did everyone on the bus, thought there was and told us to ask Donald (the bus driver) on the way off the bus. Sure enough Donald, a very nice man, told us there was a bus, although we would have to change buses at Glendaruel. We were experts by now at this sort of thing, having done it once, and looked forward to it with relish.

We said goodbye to the people on the bus and the driver Donald, a lovely silver haired driver, who was taking the bus on to Portavadie-a tiny place where you can get a ferry to Tarbert, which is a different place from Tarbet, where we stopped on our first trip and were unable to get a pint.

The sun was splitting the coconuts, so we went into the hotel the bus stopped at, got a couple of pints and asked the barman if there was somewhere we could enjoy them in the sunshine. He said there was nowhere attached to the hotel, but we could go out to the front of the hotel and enjoy them there. So we took his advice slightly further and went across the street and onto the grass and sat on a bench in the sunshine looking over the Kyles of Bute to the Island of Bute. It was a glorious way to spend an hour, much better than walking about the town and boring our readers about how great a place it is.

I believe we were breaking some new Scottish Government law which forbids drinking outside. As usual, instead of punishing the tiny percentage of the people who make an arse of themselves drinking outside, our leaders stop everyone from enjoying themselves. The same has happened with the price of drink. The parliament thinks it is too cheap which causes a tiny percentage of youngsters to drink too much. So instead of stopping them doing it, simply by getting a hold of them and kicking the shit out of them, and I am serious, the massive majority of us have to suffer an increase in the price of drink. I take it the government get the extra revenue. What a load of nonsense. That is the end of today's rant.

Craig; *The hotel looked a little upmarket for the likes of us but we had no choice but to go in. The bar however was quite satisfyingly drab. I felt instantly at home. You just can't beat a good sawdust pub.*

Of course the lager went off before I could get a pint and so I had to wait a while. There's never a good time for this to happen but when you're on a timetable and in need of Hugh Tennent's remedy for all that ails you it's disastrous.

When it eventually arrived I was both shocked and stunned to find they wanted £3.00 for it.

While we were sitting at the beach, drinking our extravagantly priced beer, we noticed a bloke getting his small boat ready for sea. We toyed with the idea of hiring him to take us down to Rothesay. Fortunately we had not yet reached the state of drink where any crazy idea seems perfectly practical. Our journey would continue by bus.

The view from the front door of the Royal Hotel

Once again our journey was in two stages. The first bus picked us up right outside the hotel and took us a few miles before turning northward. Even I knew that Rothesay was due South.

After a little panic attack I realised we were picking up other passengers and would be heading south very soon. As it turned out we were also picking up another bus and another driver. It was Donald again.

John; We got on the bus at the door of the hotel an hour later, and it took us back the way we had come for a few miles before turning left and making its way to Glendaruel Primary School, which is beautifully positioned in a lovely valley. When we got there, there was another bus waiting for us to change over into. The amazing thing was that the new bus driver was the same Donald that had left us at Tighnabruaich.

We had no idea how he did it. About a dozen perfect small children came skipping out of the school and on to the bus. Donald asked us to move to the back of the bus. We think he

thought we were a couple of old perverts!
So on the way to the ferry at Colintrive, Donald took us on a beautiful journey down old roads beside the Kyles of Bute,

Craig enjoys a beer at our beach party

stopping at houses and farms to let the kids off one at a time. It was like a scene from the Sound of Music, perfect children living an idyllic life. We even heard a Scottish accent from one of them.
Donald eventually dropped the last child off and headed back to the Colintrive to Rhubodach ferry which took us to the Isle of Bute. I have been reliably informed that yard for yard, this ferry is more expensive than flying to the States on the Concorde. (the man on the earlier bus told us that). Thankfully the ferry did not crash into a farmhouse in France, so the fare was worth it.
Note; We were not asked for our ferry tickets, which really annoyed Craig in particular. It's one of Craig's ambitions to get on the ferry to Millport for nothing, but more of that on a future trip to Millport. His point was that we did not need to buy the ticket in the first place. Mind you, if we hadn't

bought a ticket, they would have asked for it.
The bus then took us from Rhubodach down through Port Bannatyne and into Rothesay, a place I have spent many a happy time in. My granny and grandpa lived there when I was young. My auntie lived there for years and now, my sister-in-law lives and drinks there. It is good to see that there is a huge amount of work going on at the pier to deepen the inner harbour to increase the number of yachts that can come into the harbour, or create a car park, if you believe some of the locals.
I assume the vast amount of money needed to carry out this work is coming from Europe or the Lottery. We visited two pubs in the town, the first one, 'The Glue Pot' was owned for many years by my pal Robin, but he sold it recently, as he is past bus pass age, and it is not the same place anymore.
Rothesay now has a population which can be no more than about a couple of thousand, but in the small area of the town centre there are twelve pubs that I can think of, without the other small hotel bars and restaurants. This must be a record for any town?
I am amazed that Rothesay has been hit by the recession. I was asking a friend of mine, who knows someone who works in the local chemist, what percentage of prescriptions are paid for. He told me about 3%. There are so few people working on the island that I was sure it would escape the worst of the recession, but there you go.
After the obligatory fish supper, we boarded the 6.15pm ferry to Wemyss Bay. It was a lovely evening and we sat out the back of the ferry enjoying the sun and a can of lager. No draught, but toilets on the ferries.
Craig; *The journey to Rothesay was very pleasant. We even drove along the B road I had cycled up a few years back. Donald let us off conveniently close to John's favourite pub,*

The 'Glue Pot' in Rothesay (my pal Robin's old pub)

The Glue Pot. We had a beer there and another somewhere else then decided we needed food. After much thought we once again settled for a fish supper. It turned out to be one of the best I've had in ages. However having to listen to the lunatic ranting of the guy who served us took a bit of the shine off the experience.

If the Raving Loony Party ever feel like contesting the Parliamentary seat there I could suggest a prime candidate for them.

John; The two new ferries, the Bute and Argyle are huge. They hold over 50 cars each and are great for sitting in and admiring the scenery, but the locals are worried about their ability to get into Wemyss Bay when the wind is coming from a certain direction, what direction it is, I am not certain. They are so big, the wind will catch the sides and make berthing in high winds difficult. That is the end of the technical jargon, back to the trip.

Our gin palace awaits at Rothesay pier

Craig; *The ferry over to Wemyss Bay took about twenty minutes to cross giving us just enough time for a quick beer. John spent most of the train journey up to Glasgow sleeping while I spent most of my time swatting midges. It was an uneven struggle as there were several thousand more of them than me.*

John; We walked up the pier to the platform to catch the train, with a toilet, to Glasgow. I always remember when I was young, how beautiful Wemyss Bay Station was with hanging baskets of flowers everywhere. There should be money made available to allow country and coastal stations to be decorated in a way that would give pleasure to thousands of travellers. Maybe the money saved by not painting Gaelic names on ferries could be used. Mind you, the two Gaelic speakers in the country would be mad.

A beer on the ocean wave

Talking about lost languages and flowers, why are the names of flowers in Latin in garden centres? nobody can read Latin! Why not put the names in Gaelic so two people in the country can read them? That will be my last slagging off of the Gaelic community, but not the Scottish Parliament.

I believe the 50 minute train journey to Glasgow Central was very nice, but as I was asleep most of the journey, I have little to report.

Craig; *It is at this point that my story starts to differ from John's, and I'm fairly certain I know the reason why. According to John we repeated part of our previous journey by visiting the Horse Shoe bar. Not to my recollection. At one point during our travels, or to be precise during one of our refreshment breaks, John had substituted a large glass of red wine for his standard pint of sarsaparilla. This never ends well as it doesn't tend to be a great mixer with beer. On the odd occasion when I've had a couple of glasses of wine*

along with a beer my memory has also suffered, at least I think it has. I can't really remember.
Anyway, we did in fact have another drink in Glasgow but, it was in the upstairs bar in Central Station. The best I can say about this bar is that at least they keep the lighting low. Perhaps if they made the bar area look a little less like a works canteen and maybe if they painted the place some colour other than beige it would be worth a visit. Maybe if it was brightened up a bit people would be able to remember being in it.

Wemyss Bay Station, with the no hanging baskets

Our journey was rounded off, as usual, by a couple of drinks in the Monty in East Kilbride. This time we managed to get a lift up the road as Irene volunteered to come down for us, after a great sob story by yours truly. I think we were well past the strolling stage by that point.

It had been yet another great days travelling, combining the three elements of a traditional Scottish day trip. We travelled on a few buses then we had a wee sail on a boat and we made frequent stops for light refreshments.

John; Arriving in Glasgow refreshed, the rest of our trip (and most of our future trips) was like our first trip, two pints in the Horse Shoe, train to East Kilbride, two pints in the Montgomery and home to bed.

Spends for the day;

Bus Fares	Zero
Train fares	£3.80
Ferry Fares	£7.90
Food	£5.00 (fish supper)
Drink	£25.00
Total	**£41.70**

The Great Ballachulish Balls up

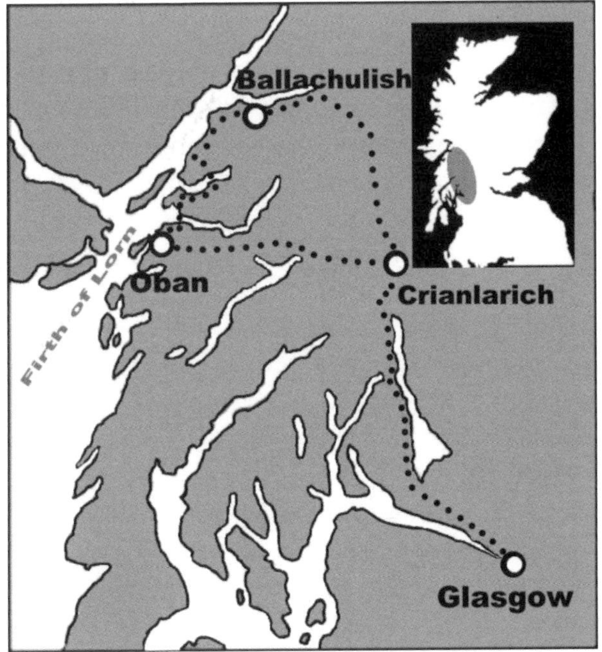

Glasgow-Glencoe & Ballachulish-Oban-Glasgow
(Three Buses-not including East Kilbride to Glasgow)

John; As you can see from above, we have decided that if we are starting our trip by going into Glasgow, we will assume by now that you know the route, walk to EK station and train into Glasgow.
When I arranged this trip, the worrying part was the final almost three hour bus run from Oban to Glasgow, so I checked that there was a train we could take if there was no, or broken, toilet on the bus. I was assuming a minimum of four pints being consumed by then.

The first thing that struck us on walking through Glasgow Central was the number of young people wearing green wellies. It was only when we arrived at Buchanan Street Bus Station, where there were more of the green wellies, we realized that as they were obviously not farmers, some were smiling, turns out they were youngsters on their way back from 'T in the Park', which finished yesterday (Sunday). As all the wellies were clean, the weather must have been good. So we reckoned some smart entrepreneur probably made a killing ripping off the kids by giving them crap weather reports so they would all buy wellies.
Funnily enough, since then Kate (the wife) has told me of a girl she knew who bought a pair of the green wellies, but when she opened the parcel discovered that they were two left feet, so she immediately applied for a place in Scotland's football squad.
When we got to the bus stance, there were dozens of people there and it ended up that, although we had booked seats (50p each), we could not get seats together, and could therefore not sneak a piece on the journey (I couldn't get corned beef out of my mind).
A thing that really annoyed us was that there were at least four people sitting opposite who knew each other, but all took window seats, so they all had strangers sitting next to them and I missed Craig's riveting conversation on the journey! A shower of dunderheads.
Craig; *John's latest planed adventure, our third, was to take us on a journey up through historic Glencoe and on to Oban before returning to Glasgow. It meant sitting on a bus for far longer than we had before and, more importantly, it meant less access to the reviving liquids to be found at our rest stops. For me it would be a test of character as I am rather fond of those reviving liquids.*

Senior citizen's travel club?

We arrived at the bus station in Glasgow with plenty of time to spare. In fact we were, or at least should have been, first in the queue. That's not how it turned out. With so much time on our hands I decided to visit the shop. That was possibly a mistake on my part. Not only did I not find anything I wanted to buy but, by the time I got back to the bus stance a fair crowd of passengers had arrived for the Glencoe bus. Worse still they were all much more travel savvy than us. It never occurred to us that on such a scenic trip all the window seats would be nabbed by the seasoned travellers. Sitting in an aisle seat beside a total stranger was not the way I thought I would be travelling. It gave me something to seethe over as we made our way through Glasgow. There's nothing quite like a good seethe to get you through the day.

The route we were travelling followed the same path as our first journey for a while. As we entered Tarbet I remembered to look over at the bus stop we had waited at for the phantom McGill's bus. I fully expected to see a couple of old geezers pacing up and down, occasionally glaring along the road. There was no one waiting there, not even a pair of irate codgers.

John; Although it was a dull and misty day, the journey up Loch Lomond, passing the Tarbet Hotel where we couldn't get a pint on our first journey, was lovely.

After Tarbet, the A82 is very narrow and winding and clings to the side of the loch, very dramatic, unless you are a cyclist. We passed the Drovers Inn where Kate and I have spent a couple of nights. A tip here. If any of our readers want to book a room there, ask for the rooms across the road from the Inn. The rooms in the Inn are beyond belief, not in a good way, but they are clean. The building is so old and twisted that you can leave the room without opening the door. But it is a great place with a fantastic bar and great food.

And so the bus carried on up to Crianlarich, which is a tiny place with a station and a T junction, although all junctions in the North of Glasgow mention it by name. When I was young, before I ventured up north, I always thought it must be a big place. It was up then through Bridge of Orchy to Glencoe, passing the lay-by with the piper to amuse the tourists and the ubiquitous hot dog stands, really Scottish!

Glencoe is an amazing place in any weather with The Three Sisters dominating the start. The Three Sisters in Glencoe, like their counterparts in the Blue Mountains near Sydney (eat your heart out Bill Bryson), are giant pieces of cold forbidding granite that makes my blood freeze. My wife has two sisters, by the way. I don't know how they came into my mind there.

Craig; *Being born and bred in Ayrshire I am not easily impressed by what passes for outstanding scenery to some people. As we travelled along our route towards Glencoe I was a little less than taken with what was on show. In many places it was hard to see very much of anything to be honest. It would appear that the Forestry Commission have taken it upon itself to obscure what scenery there is. For mile after mile of what should have been outstanding natural beauty the only thing on show was a large, jaggy, green wall of pine trees. It is incredible that they have been allowed to get away with scarring the countryside like this. I expect they'll be planting wind turbines here soon. Not that I'm against windmills, I quite like them, just not a hundred or so at a time.*

Things changed dramatically at the entrance to the glen. The weather had been a bit depressing up till then, with mist and low cloud always threatening to stop us enjoying any of the scenic grandeur we were so hell bent on appreciating. Almost any landscape is improved by a bit of sunshine but I think Glencoe would look magnificent whatever the weather, the sun coming out just made it even more stunning.

Glencoe is of course most famous for the massacre which happened there in 1692. The historical background to it has always been a bit controversial. Some claim it was a political strategy aimed at subduing the Jacobites. Others say it was just clan rivalry. Either way what really marked this out as a terrible crime was the fact that The Campbell's had enjoyed the highland hospitality of the McDonald clan before turning on them.

I have my own theory. It was quite simply an extreme reaction to a miserly full Scottish breakfast. After enduring 12 days of highland hospitality the Campbell's just snapped, it could happen to anyone. I've never stayed in the

Highlands for more than a few days at a time, but I can understand what they were having to put up with. The constant midge attacks and the stingy portions of food, not to mention the service all add up to mitigating circumstances.

Back to the present day and we were about to find out that hospitality is still a bit thin on the ground in Glencoe. Once in the village I was just about to suggest to John that we should get off the bus to take in the sights when I noticed that the Glencoe Hotel was all boarded up, this is rarely a good sign. Getting the feel of the place, immersing yourself in the history of such an iconic part of Scotland's heritage is all very well, but when they shut the only pub that's just a right bugger.

Needless to say we remained on the bus. A few minutes later we arrived at the Ballachulish Hotel. The hotel seemed a wee bit fancy, all armchairs and brushed aluminium. Most of the bar staff, two out of three to be precise, had recently arrived from Eastern Europe. That seems to be the way of things in the Scottish hotel trade. I'm not complaining. The service is much better, even if you are never quite sure your 'patter' is really appreciated. Lost in translation is the phrase which springs to mind. Another draw back is that when you ask your barman about local buses and or services you're unlikely to get much useful information. Then again maybe that's not much different from what you could expect from some of the locals we've met.

John's meticulous planning meant we had time for two pints in the hotel. His standing as an expedition leader took rather a knock however when the next part of his master plan fell apart. Our bus down to Oban was to be a Citylink coach which would have to cross the Ballachulich Bridge. This meant we would be able to see it coming in plenty of time. That bus never appeared but another one did and it nearly caught us unawares. Where it came from I have no idea. I do know it wasn't a Citylink bus and it certainly didn't come across the bridge.

The 'Busless' Ballachulish Bridge

John; We made our way through the Glen, past the village of Glencoe, the bus stopped at the now closed Glencoe Hotel, an unbelievably ugly building.

You know the type of building, built just after concrete was invented.

We got off our bus just before it went over the Ballachulish Bridge, down a set of stairs and into the Hotel of the same name. It is a lovely hotel and built to complement the fabulous scenery, not ruin it. We enjoyed a couple of pints while enjoying the view over Loch Leven. We went outside and enjoyed our pieces across the road at the edge of the loch, magic.

We had (after double checking) planned to catch the 14.18pm Citylink bus from outside the hotel. I decided to visit the toilets in the hotel (which were, by the way, great) before we got on the bus. This was not a problem as Craig would be able to see the bus approach over the bridge, as it was coming from Fort William, so I told Craig not to worry about it suddenly appearing out of nowhere before I returned.

Just as I came out of the Hotel, a West Coast Coach suddenly appeared out of nowhere, going to Oban, where we were going. As this was 20 minutes after our bus should have arrived, we managed to stop it and get on, and not have to pay. It's all a bit worrying. On every journey we have been on, different buses turn up out of the blue. Never mind, they're all free.

The bus to Oban goes along the coast passing down the end of Loch Linnie and the Firth of Lorn, passing lots of small islands, and lovely small villages with nice restaurants and bars. Although the day was very misty you could see (or couldn't see) it was a lovely journey.

We crossed the Connel Bridge and headed into Oban, arriving later than we should have, at 15.30pm.

Craig; *The scenery on the road down to Oban was amazing. I just wish I could remember the names of the places we travelled through and of the odd ancient castle we passed by. The last time I visited Oban was a couple of years ago and it didn't go well. The Tourist Information Office in the town proved anything but informative back then and things didn't seem to be much better now. We had a bit of bother finding the bus station and no one could tell us where it was. There seemed to be a shortage of signs or maybe the locals have hidden them all. That would be one way of keeping the tourists in the town. I can't think of any other reason for staying in Oban. By now were getting desperate so we asked in the Tourist Office. Grudgingly they told us where it was, they couldn't do anything else really as it was just outside their front door. Even then we didn't believe it so we asked a* *policewoman. To call it a bus station was really stretching things a bit too far. Since when does three bus shelters randomly placed along the pavement constitute a bus station.*

By the time we were certain where we were meant to catch our next bus we only had time for a single quick drink, yet another reason for not liking Oban. The Caledonian Hotel was a bit too posh looking for my liking and it obviously went to John's head. Instead of the usual common as muck pint of slops he opted for a glass of fine red wine, or as I like to call it John's sleeping potion. The mist had come down by the time we got on our bus, making Oban more miserable looking than usual. I wasn't sad to be leaving.

John; Before heading for a pint, we tried to find out where we got the Citylink 16.10pm bus to Glasgow. There was no timetable or mention of such a service in the bus station and no bus person to ask, so we stopped a policeman and lady policewoman. The policewoman knew the details of the bus and where it left from. I was amazed and asked her how she knew all this, to be told that her husband was a bus driver for Citylink. I asked her if he was ever home on time at night.

We did not have much time left to look for a decent pub, so we went across the road into the Caledonian Hotel, another one of these big hotels that were build for a bygone era. There is no atmosphere in these places, but we had a nice view out to the ferry terminal and saw a couple of these huge roll on roll off ferries coming and going to the islands which were hiding in the mist.

Worrying about missing our bus, although we were certain it would be late, if it turned up at all, I looked out the window to see it sitting at the bus stop waiting for us, amazing! We dived out and got our free ticket from a torn faced driver, not the policewoman's husband (I asked). There was a working

Oban lost in the mist (we should be so lucky)

toilet on the bus, everything was perfect, apart from only having one pint in Oban.

I have not mentioned much about Oban. It's called 'The Gateway to the Islands'. I have been there before. It always seems to be cold and blowing a gale.

Maybe that's why it's called the gateway to the western islands, everybody who arrives there wants to get through the gate as soon as possible.

Our bus left on time and headed through more lovely scenery until it arrived at Tyndrum. The daft thing is that it stopped in a lay by a good bit past the area where there were touristy things and places to buy a drink. The driver told us we were stopping for ten minutes, but that it was a five minute walk back to the shops so we were not to try it as he would leave us. Can you imagine what real tourists must think. The only reason he stopped was to have a smoke.

Anyway, we left after he had a smoke and the run back down Loch Lomond and into Glasgow was lovely. We arrived back in Glasgow at 7.00pm.

On the road to nowhere

We had the usual two pints in the Horse Shoe Bar and got the 40p train back to East Kilbride and into the Monty. Kate text'd me and offered to pick us up from the Monty. What a woman, and a lucky one too!

Craig; *Our trip back down to Glasgow was much better than I had expected. Probably because I managed to get some sleep for once. I woke up just as we drove into Tyndrum but I was a little confused when the bus didn't actually stop in the village. Whoever planned the timetable for this section of the route must have a serious character flaw. After having his passengers sitting on the bus for an hour or so this genius has timetabled the first, and only, stop for a lay-by half a mile away from any services. Not exactly a comfort stop. Unless of course you happen to be a fag smoking bus driver. Once again I found time to have a good seethe.*

The rest of the trip was fairly uneventful. We managed a couple of brews in the Horse Shoe and a couple more in the Monty before ending our latest adventure.

John; You will have noticed that I have stopped slagging off the Gaelic speaking people. The reason for this is that my youngest son Gregor (I have three sons of different ages) works in a film production company in Glasgow, and much of his time is working on Gaelic programmes, so he told me that if it was not for the two Gaelic speakers he might be out of a job. So no more slagging the Gaelic world.
One of my normal ranting views was confirmed on this trip, that is that most (but not all) Scots who work in the tourist related industry, including transport, are miserable bastards. But our Policewomen are great.

Spends for the day;

Bus fares	£0.50 (to book seats, which we didn't get)
Train fares	£0.80 (return EK to Glasgow)
Food	Zero (had no food, only pieces
Drink	£22.00
Total	**£23.30**

Stranraer-a Town too Far

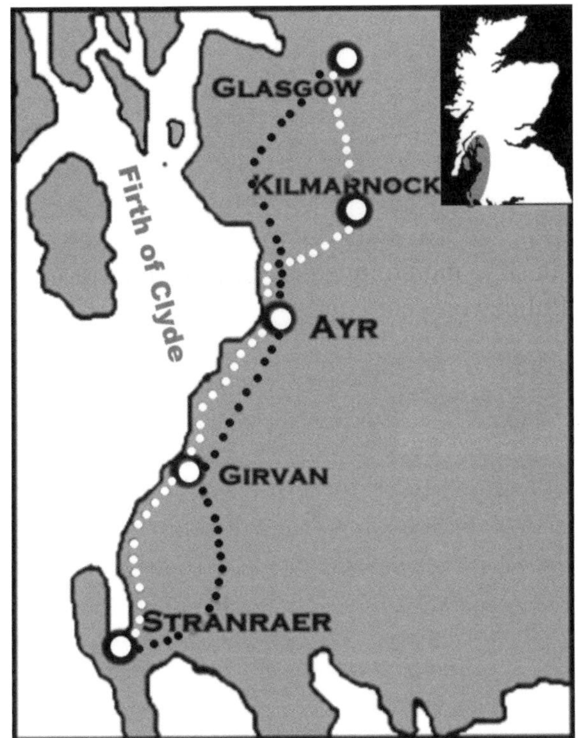

East Kilbride-Ayr-Girvan-Stranraer-Glasgow -East Kilbride
(Three Buses, Two Trains)

John; This was our first trip on a Friday, the first three were Monday trips. I was glad as it had a fairly late finish and I could have a long lie on Saturday. As it happened, Kate was going on holiday to Majorca that day with her two sisters. Luckily, they had a very early start so I was able to drive them to Prestwick before our trip started.

The first stagecoach out of town

This also meant that I would return to an empty house, so Kate would not know how many pints I would have had!
For the first time on a trip, we left from EK bus station on the X16, which goes to Ayr via Kilmarnock, Prestwick Airport and Prestwick. The bus was one of the brand new double deckers, so it was straight upstairs for a lovely run to Ayr. It was funny passing Prestwick where I had dropped of "*the three sisters*" earlier that morning.
Craig gave me a lot of interesting information on the way, he used to live and work in the Kilmarnock/Ayr area. The best information he had was the name and location of a great wee pub in Ayr called The Bridges Bar.
There was a great wee crowd of people of our age inside and everyone was friendly and talkative. One of the interesting facts we learned about that area of Ayr was that the Ladies of the Night used to put the price of a short time with them on the soles of there feet. This seemed so crazy that I assumed it must be true. We learned other interesting facts as we downed a couple of pints, and very enjoyable they were. Amazing how drink tastes better on a Friday than a Monday.

It was then back to Ayr Bus Station for the next bus to take us to Girvan. It arrived on time, everything was running smoothly so far. How long would it last?

Craig; *Trip number four. Today's journey started out from East Kilbride bus station from where we would travel down to Ayr then on to Girvan before arriving in the town of Stranraer. I was very impressed by the bus service down to Ayr. This service is covered by Stagecoach West Scotland. Although there were no Indian attacks on our stagecoach there were a few hostiles circling it in Kilmarnock. They were definitely palefaces, but, they were hooded rather than masked. In the end they didn't even get on to our bus. I found that quite surprising as it seems to me that if you were forced to live in Kilmarnock you would be unlikely to pass up a chance to hop on a bus leaving town. That's probably a bit harsh, but if the bus station is anything to go by things must be getting a bit grim down in old Killie.*

Sitting upstairs in our luxurious double-decker bus we had a great view of the magnificent Ayrshire countryside. Did I mention I'm from Ayrshire? The bus didn't seem to be speeding along at all but we arrived at our destination after only an hour and a quarter.

Once in Ayr I was able to give John the benefit of all my experience, gained over many years, over forty I think, visiting the towns' hotspots. Since we only had an hour or so to spend in Ayr we decided to scamper along the street to one of the towns most famous hostelries, Bridges Bar.

All the way down on the bus I was getting more and more worried. My problem was that I hadn't been into Bridges Bar for years. I was worried that the bar could have suffered the same fate as other good traditional Scottish pubs, refurbishment. That is the process of ripping out all the original fixtures and fittings and replacing them with plastic

versions of the exact same thing, then installing children behind the bar to serve. These modernised pubs tend to look as if they have been redesigned by the Disney Corporation.
My worries were unfounded. Bridges Bar was just as I remembered it, well worn and lived in. I doubt there are any major fittings in the place that weren't there back in the 1980's when I last visited. Apart from the lack of a smokescreen, thanks again to the Scottish Parliament, time had stood still.
It's a pity the same couldn't be said of the patrons. Like me, and John, time hasn't been too kind to the drinkers in this great little pub. But when you get to certain age you appreciate a well run boozer. In Bridges you get just that, good beer, reasonably priced, and a friendly atmosphere. The range of topics discussed in your average no frills pub would amaze the uninitiated. In the space of an hour or so all the world's problems can be solved.

Bridges Bar

The tricky thing I always find is remembering the solutions the next day, or even later in the session.
We were lucky, I suppose, to come into the conversation at a late stage. The assembled drinkers had already worked their way through the mundane stuff like geopolitical instabilities and such like and had reached the really gritty stage of today's agenda. That revolved around a question of Ayr's cultural heritage, namely listed buildings and brothels. At one point the owner insisted, straight faced, that one particular listed building he knew of was being used as a brothel. Not only that but the ladies of the house had their services and charges written on the soles of their shoes. I just wonder how they managed to keep their balance when they were showing the menu to prospective customers. Maybe our storyteller just saw a price tag on some young lady's shoe and jumped to the wrong conclusion.
After two rather fine pints and a little more insane chatter we returned to the bus station where John was immediately in his element. He discovered a display rack with 30 odd timetables to collect. Our good mood evaporated once we got aboard our bus to Girvan.
A ned and his lady got on and sat in the seat just in front of us. I'm fairly certain that'll be the first and last time she's ever been referred to in those terms. They were unbelievable. Talk about stereotypes, Rab C Nesbit would have come across as a upper-class toff compared to them.
They were both dressed in designer gear. What intrigues me is that couch potatoes like these always wear sports gear, why? Where do they get the money for it? Who washes it for them? They didn't look fit enough to walk the length of themselves never mind run a marathon. I'm pretty sure they would have a stroke if required to do anything energetic. They certainly didn't seem capable of a stroke of work.

It's hard to say what was most objectionable about this pair, their eating habits, their drinking or just the fact that they got on our bus. Almost as soon as they got on they started wolfing down a fast food carry-out. I couldn't make out which country's cuisine was getting the ned taste test, it was disappearing too fast. They then proceeded to wash the food down with a carefully selected bottle of wine. Presumably selected for its bouquet and it's price of under £3.00. I thought the brown paper bag was a classy touch. The girl, possibly the ugliest person I've seen this side of a channel 5 documentary, was with child. Now I have a very creative imagination I'm told, but I couldn't begin to speculate on what would be the outcome of mixing the genes of these two specimens. Steven King might be interested in the film rights. Suffice it to say I'm now in favour of some sort of licence to breed. In this case I think we would have to say, ' Licence Revoked'.

I was ever so glad when they got off in Maybole. Having visited it a couple of times I'm sure they'll fit right in. The rest of the journey was enjoyable and again rather quick.

John; The weather was lovely again and we had a lovely run down the coast, passing through tiny villages I never knew existed. We also passed Turnberry Hotel where I have spent many a happy time in the Hotel and on the Golf course. Always on expenses. Can't afford it now, unfortunately.

We arrived safely in Girvan and as we had a couple of hours there Craig showed me the harbour where he spent many a happy hour when he was a boy.

We made our way across the street to the imaginatively named Harbour Bar. This was another old mans' pub and we had a couple of pints there. The only thing of interest I can remember was that the pub seemed to be used as a toilet and

baby changing area for a very young mother. That apart it was an enjoyable couple of pints.
We then left for a wee walk to find out where we got on the next bus. We had no luck so we went into another pub. This was a fancy one with a restaurant and a lovely beer garden overlooking the harbour, so we had pint there. We were given vague instructions about where to get our next bus, and as we were both mellow by this time, we stupidly believed the barman.
So we left the bar and made our way to where we thought we would get our bus. After walking for about ten minutes we realized we were on the wrong road, and since the time for our bus had passed, we mentally gave up and turned a corner to take us back into Girvan. Amazingly, as we passed a stop, our bus appeared. At least it did to Craig. I had taken my lenses out and couldn't see anything close up.
Craig; *Girvan was just as I remembered it, and that's probably not a good thing given I'm talking about 20 odd years ago. After a quick look around the harbour we entered a great little bar. The décor was straight out of the 1970's, all wood panelling and tartan carpets. The clientele was of the same vintage. I include John and myself in that grouping. The barman, possibly the owner, was in fine form chatting and joking with his customers. It must be an Ayrshire thing, this warm and welcoming attitude in pubs. Have I mentioned that I once worked in a bar in Ayrshire? A couple of drinks later we decided to take in a few more of the sights of the town. Ten minutes later we found it necessary to enter The Roxy, in an attempt to find out some vital travel information you understand.*
By this time the sun was out and things were getting hot, so hot in fact that we decided some liquids were urgently needed. Luckily for us the Roxy had a very nice beer garden.

Turnberry Hotel taken from speeding and bumpy bus

After we had ordered our drinks we asked the barman for directions to our next bus stop. It didn't seem to me to be a very hard question but you never can tell.

The main stumbling block was getting the boy behind the bar to understand the spoken word. It would seem that many bars employ university students as staff during the summer months. I've never quite worked out why. Certainly they work for minimum wage but many of them seem to have minimum usefulness, they are clueless. Common sense apparently isn't on the curriculum of our leading sites of learning. The would be captain of industry we asked for directions managed to send us along the wrong street to our next bus stop. When you consider there were only two roads to choose from you begin to get the impression that this young man is never going to be leading a research team.

I'm beginning to see a pattern developing. It seems if you want some local knowledge the last person to ask is a local.

Once again we were forced into a strength sapping march along the road. Time was ticking bye and bus stops were so thin on the ground they didn't actually exist. John had planned most of the route with military precision but this part was unknown territory for us. Long before we got to the end of the road we realised that we had been led astray and would be missing our bus to Stanraer. There was nothing else for it but to turn back into town, once we turned the corner at the end of the road. Our plan would then be to sit in the pub for an unspecified period of time before travelling back to Glasgow by train. I was devastated at the thought. You can imagine how surprised we were when we got round the corner just in time to see our bus, fashionably late, coming down the street towards us.

We spent the next twenty minutes laughing and congratulating each other on how smart and or lucky we had been. Then John fell asleep. I on the other hand kept vigil, except for a couple of minutes as we passed through Cairnryan and it's ferry port. If you know Cairnryan you'll understand how that could have happened. In Stranraer we made a rookie mistake by once again asking a local for directions. When will we ever learn? I couldn't understand a word he said. Being a good soul I nodded and smiled, pretending his help had just about made my day.

John; After sitting down and getting over the shock of getting the bus, we enjoyed our run down to Stranraer. We had our pieces on the bus as nobody could see us, and corned beef does not smell much, another great thing about my favourite piece filling.

We arrived at Stranraer, had a walk around the town and front and immediately realized it would have been better if we had missed the bus. It is the most ugly and depressing place I have ever seen.

Thankfully, for we had three hours to kill before we got the train home, we found a great, and very cheap pub called 'The Commercial Inn'. Years ago every town had a Commercial Inn. Two pints were only about £3.60, although we found out later it was the happy hour from four till seven every Friday. What a great idea. After a couple of very happy hours in the company of some of the hardest men I have ever met, and as I come from Govan and Craig from Auchinleck, that is saying something. We said our goodbyes and went to find a chip shop. We got our fish suppers, which were delicious. So although Stranraer is a dump, it has a great pub and chip shop. What more can you ask for. We then nicked into one of these small versions of big supermarkets and got a couple of cans each for the train journey home. Trains are great with toilets and everything.
We made our way down to the station, which is beside the ferry terminal, eating our fish suppers.
Craig; *It is no exaggeration to say that Stranraer, on first impression, looks like an asylum seekers transit camp. Not that there were lots of people milling around trying to get into the country, more likely the other way round. In fact there were hardly any people around at all. This seems a little strange when you realise that Stranraer is an entry and exit point for the UK. Many thousands of people travel through the port every year, perhaps a decent pub or two would slow them down a bit. Given it's mostly Irish and Scots using the ferry the lack of a passable boozer seems like a major oversight. After a bit of a false start we found a pub, and from the outside it looked anything but a decent one. As it turned out it wasn't too bad. The Commercial didn't look to be any great shakes on the inside either. My opinion of the place was about to change dramatically. When I discovered that we had only been charged £3.60 for two*

pints of beer I was almost moved to tears. We made a big thing about it, telling the locals we had to pay almost twice as much up in Glasgow. They seemed genuinely shocked by this. It turned out they were taking the pish. It was 'happy hour' in the Commercial. Years from now they'll still be talking about the day they pulled one over on them there city folks. I suppose it's better than putting unwary tourists into a 'wicker man'.

Apart from having a peculiar sense of humour the pub patrons were very friendly. We even got directions to the railway station from one of the older bar-flies. This time

Last chance saloon

they were more or less accurate. The same can't be said for his claim that there was a bar in the station. Maybe the old boy hadn't used the train in the last few decades but, there was no sign of any bar.

As you can imagine we were less than impressed with this state of affairs. Fortunately John had a back-up plan. At his insistence we had bought a small carry out for the train. We spent a good part of the journey home hiding our cans under the table in case the conductor caught us. That's what happens when two old guys go travelling. We were still thinking things were like the old days. Nowadays no one gives a bugger. Everyone else on the train was slurping away at their hooch quite openly, without a care in the world.

Once again we finished off our days' travel with a final beer in the Monty.

Down in the mouth down south

I like to think of this part of our journey as a time to reflect on the day's experiences. John likes to think of it as a time to top up our 'beer tanks'. either way, it's a great way to wind up yet another of our adventures.

John; We had about half an hour to kill, so we watched the sea view, which is depressing, and the ferries sailing about.
The journey back to Glasgow was a beautiful journey, the equal of any in the world. I would encourage anyone from Stranraer to make the journey-just make sure it's a one way journey! We passed through a lot of Craig's old stamping grounds and he has assured me he is glad the old stamping days are behind him. He gave me a running commentary on places we passed through in Galloway and Ayrshire where you're better off staying on the train-and there were quite a lot of them. I'm sure the real reason he was going on was to try and keep me conscious. We enjoyed our two cans and never needed to go to the toilet. When it's there, you don't need to go.
It was about ten o'clock when we arrived in Glasgow, so we did not go to the Horseshoe, but got the 10.12 train back to EK and headed straight to the Monty for a wee swally before closing time.
I'm not sure how many pints we had in the Monty, and Kate was not in to tell me, but we had another great day in the South West of Scotland.
Spends for the day;

Bus fares	zero
Train fares	£11.00 approx.
Food	£5.00 (fish supper)
Drink	£30.00 approx. (including carry out)
Total	**£46.00**

(will have to cut out some of the bevy)

A Ferry Nice Day

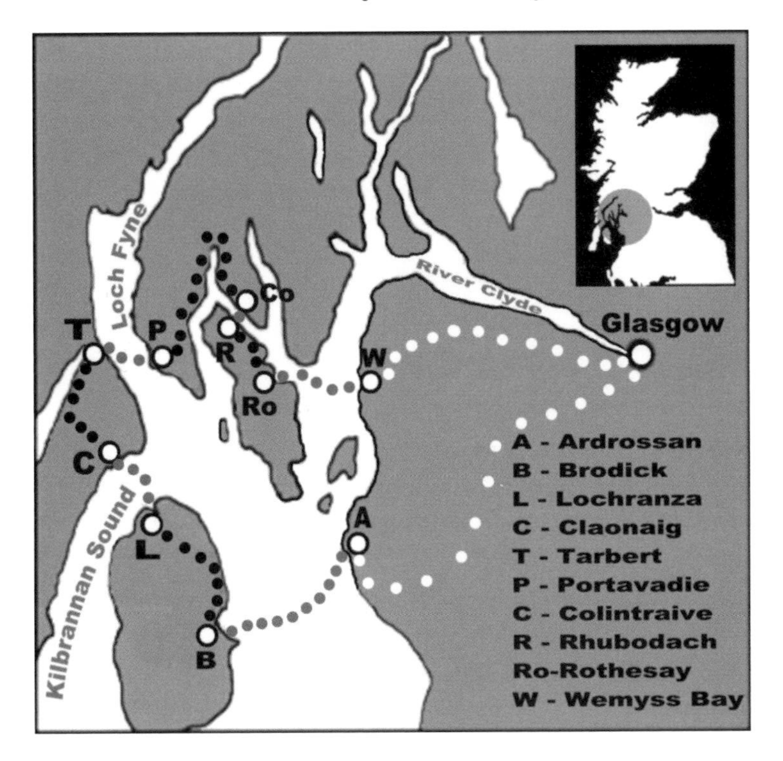

East Kilbride-Glasgow-Ardrossan-Brodick-Lochranza -Cloanaig-Tarbert-Portavadie-Rothesay- Wemyss Bay-Glasgow-East Kilbride
(Three Buses, Five Ferries, Four Trains)

John; As you can see from above, this was a very busy trip which did not include many free buses, so it was an expensive trip. However we were looking forward to all the ferry journeys. The day started with Irene giving us a run down to the station. This was a great, and free way to start the journey . However, as it was a very early start,

Pottering around platform 11a

with the train for Glasgow leaving at 7.47am, I did not get any discount on the train ticket to Ardrossan, but Craig did, as he is disabled all day, but I am just old after 9.00am.

It was an express train into Glasgow which only stopped at two instead of the usual eight stations, so we could not work out why it took roughly the same time. We got a bit of a shock on the way into the station when we spotted an Ardrossan train leaving. However, all was well as there was one leaving at 8.33am as I had planned.

The train left from platform 11a. It was like the Harry Potter film. The platform was so far away we nearly missed the damn train.

Our discussions on the train centred round whether or not the bar on the ferry to Brodick would be open as it left at 9.45am. I was the most nautically experienced (I have my 'Day Skipper' Certificate) and was sure it would be open. We arrived at Ardrossan on time and bought our five ferry island hopscotch ticket. No discount and £16 down the swanny. I suppose it is reasonable for five ferry journeys, especially as the bar opened as soon as we cast off. The ferry

was packed with golfers and some American tourists. We were wondering what they thought about every man on the Ferry having a pint at 10.00am. They were all on diet coke, but were all fat. Early drinking is definitely a West of Scotland thing.
The views from the windows of the bar were excellent, although it was a misty and dull day, and it stayed that way for most of the day.
Craig; *September can be a bit dodgy for travelling round Scotland, weather wise. Sometimes you can be lucky and get a nice sunny, warm day. More likely it is the showery, overcast, limited visibility variety. Our latest day out fell into the latter category. Anyone who knows the island of Arran will not be surprised to learn that it was a little bit cold and watery while we were there.*
We had a saying back in my old home town which rather sums up the peculiar climate. When standing at the highest vantage point in the town it was said that if you couldn't see the isle of Arran on the horizon it meant it was raining there. However if you could see it that meant it was about to rain.
Although it didn't exactly pour at any time during our journey round the Clyde Estuary, due to mist, the scenic grandeur of the area was a bit more implied than apparent. We could have been anywhere in Scotland.
The trip really began at Central Station in Glasgow. We arrived there in plenty of time and I have to say I was very surprised to find our next destination and it's platform number were already displayed on the big board. Usually the underachiever in charge of the board waits to the last possible minute before informing the long suffering public that their train is about to leave from the furthest away platform.

Craig on the deck of the Arran Ferry

.

It can't be a bundle of laughs sitting in a wee darkened room typing out train times all day so maybe the poor souls deserve a little understanding. If you'll pardon the pun, perhaps it keeps them from going off the rails.
As it was the platform number for the Ardrossan train was given as 11A. That sounded a little Harry Potterish to me but there really was such a platform. I have to report that it was far from magical.
The ferry left Ardrossan bang on time at 9.45am and John's mind turned immediately to the most crucial question of the day: when does the bar open? He bet me that the bar would open as soon as we cleared the harbour. I explained to him that since Arran was visible from the mainland, on a clear day at least, you could hardly claim to be in international waters. Not for the last time I lost a bet with John. The bar was indeed open. We thought that was worth celebrating so we went in for a couple of beers.

It's always time for beer

As you can imagine we were in Brodick before we knew it. It was only a few yards from the harbour to the bus stance so John didn't get much of a chance to take in the sights, such as they were. We only had a few minutes to find the bus which would take us up to Lochranza in the north of Arran.

There are only three bus routes on the island, north circular, south circular and the one across the middle. That, you would imagine, would make life simple for passengers and of course for the compiler of the bus timetables.

Island people have a different outlook on life to mainlanders. They work to a different logic. This concept can be seen in their attitude to sign posting. The good folk of Arran appear to think that everyone knows where the buses are going to and therefore see no reason to display their destinations. Our bus, on the north circular route, had the phrase 'Bus for Hire' displayed where you would normally find a place name.

I have to say most people did seem to know where it was going, except for the two people in front of us who were getting into a bit of a panic about it.

There also doesn't seem to be a maximum capacity for buses on the island. We were moved up the bus as more and more passengers got on board. There are buses in India with more elbow room than our bus up to Lochranza.

John; We arrived at Brodick on time and alighted with the tourists on their way to the Whisky or Cheese trails, or to play golf. We only just managed to get on the bus to Lochranza and had to stand till the tourists got off at one of the cheese places. The journey to Lochranza was very hilly and Craig kept reminding me that he had cycled and walked this road, although I cannot think why when there are perfectly good buses which are free.

When we got off at Lochranza we found a very nice seat looking over to the Kintyre Peninsula and ate our pieces (normal filling for me) as our ferry approached. Although dull it was dry and very scenic. Because of our short stay here, we had no time to visit the local hotel.

***Craig;** Once again we had very little time to look around the town, just enough to eat our sandwiches. We sat on a bench eating and watching our ferry coming across from Cloanaig, our next destination.*

Just for a change I had decided to go all exotic and bought myself a couple of mini Cornish pasties. This turned out to be a step too far. They were dreadful. Actually I can only vouch for one of them being toxic as I heaved the other one on to the rocks for the seagulls to scoff. As it turned out I had vastly underestimated the dietary threshold of the common seagull. The picky buggers wouldn't touch the

pasty. This didn't do a lot for my churning stomach and I was no longer looking forward to our next sea crossing.
John; We said goodbye to Arran and got on the wee ferry which took us over to Cloanaig. It was a nice sail and we were able to stay outside and watch the scenery pass. As we approached the jetty there was no sign of a bus, but there was a bus shelter..
The bus arrived at advertised time and spent about half an hour taking us up to Tarbert. It was very misty and we could not see much. When we arrived we headed for the nearest bar.

Aboard the Marie Celeste?

After a couple of not very great pints we left and walked the short distance to the jetty to catch the 2.15pm ferry to Portavadie. It rained while we were on the ferry so we had to take shelter for a wee while.
Craig; *Once on board the ferry it was hard not to notice that the crew outnumbered the passengers. Although within a few minutes we were left alone. The other travellers had taken shelter and the crew had disappeared completely. Eventually we found out that they had all gone to the Bridge. Why, we*

could only speculate. John decided that there must be a really good card game going on up there, while I preferred the notion that they were afraid of the open sea and because they were not very experienced sailors they were all huddled together up in the wheelhouse whimpering.
Either way we somehow managed to make the crossing safely and stepped ashore looking for our next connection.
As we approached the bus stop John's instincts kicked in once more. Like a native tracker he looked around, tested the wind direction with his finger and announced that the bus would be here in a few minutes. He also predicted that the bus would be approaching from the left. Remembering his earlier prediction up in Balahulish, I immediately turned to my right, just in time to see our bus coming round the corner.
The journey from Cloanaig to Tarbert was really enjoyable. I had good reason to remember this road. I had travelled the length and occassionally the breadth of it on my bike while on one of my tours. I have to say that it is much easier, never mind quicker, by bus.
The road is single tracked for about 5 miles which makes life exciting, especially at blind corners. Luckily we didn't meet anything, not a single lumbering juggernaut, or even a wobbling, aged cyclist.
When the bus actually did stop it was outside a small isolated cottage. We were quite interested to see who would be getting on. The door opened and instead of someone getting on the driver threw a small package out of the bus and over the hedge into the garden of the little house.
Since there was no explosion we decided to give the driver the benefit of the doubt and assume that he was delivering said package and not carrying on some sort of rural feud.
The bus made a bit of a detour when it called into the

Kennacraig ferry port. It must make some sort of sense for the ferry to leave from this port but I can't fathom it myself. It's in the middle of nowhere. The ferry itself was huge, much larger than the one we had just been on. No one got off our bus and as far as we could tell there was not one single passenger to be seen around the boat, so you really must ask just how profitable this service is.

Tarbert was pretty much as I remembered it from my cycling holiday but then there isn't much you could do to change it. We had a couple of beers in a pub I'd been in last time. Good beer and not a bad pub.

Sitting there reminded me of one of the guest houses I had looked at on the internet while I was planning my trip. It advertised itself as a traditional family run well appointed house with plenty of atmosphere. Lucky for me I decided on a different house. When I actually saw the place it turned out to be opposite a fish market and the atmosphere would have stopped even the strongest stomach from holding on to the traditional Scottish breakfast.

The ferry over to Portavadie was the smallest we had been on all day, but it was a great wee journey. We stayed on deck for most of the trip, only taking shelter when the wind and rain got up a bit. The scenery was fantastic, if a wee bit fleeting.

I personally think the mist helped create a great atmosphere. Occasionally the sun would burst through the low cloud cover like the beam of a searchlight, changing the colour of the sea.

Our little ferry reached Portavadie after about 20 minutes. Once the ramp went down we could see that there was nothing to see in Portavadie. The last time I'd been there the talk about the place was all about some old boy being found dead in his nearby cottage. It was the liveliest thing

that had happened there in years.
The bus company which operates from the ferry port goes by the name of 'Wee Geoff's Bus'. I'm fairly sure that Wee Geoff himself was our driver. The wee man drove us through Tighnabruich and onto Glendaruel where we had to change buses. That's how we were reunited with Donald and his bus. Strange to say Donald didn't recognise us. We were crushed.
John; When we got off the ferry it was still raining so we took shelter in Cal Macs ferry terminal-honest, a proper wee terminal-it was magic. So was the bus when it arrived.
The bus company is called 'Wee Geoff's' Kool Bus'. If wee Geoff's' no well, there's no bus!
We were pretty sure that we would be changing buses at Glendaruel Primary School. We have done this before on a previous trip, and sure enough, when we pulled into the school grounds, there was Donald waiting in another bus to deliver the kids to their homes, which are all farms, and take us to Rothesay. As I said, we have done this part of the journey before, but you never tire of a run down into Rothesay, where we arrived at 4.30pm, and the sun came out to greet us. It was lovely.
Sheila (my sister-in-law) had planned to meet us at 5.00pm, so after a pint in The Esplanade, we walked along to meet Sheila and had another pint in the Grapes. It was 5.00pm when we went into the Grapes and there were only a few people in, but they were all drunk. The elderly barmaid asked me to dance, I must be a babe magnet! (only in Rothesay). After our hastily downed pint, we escaped and went to the Criterion for another three pints.
We had a lovely time with Sheila, who can drink even more than Craig, and that's saying something.

The troops storm ashore at Portavadie

We had to hurry to catch the seven o'clock ferry to Wemyss Bay. It was a great sail over to Wemyss Bay, I had a 'Lecky Bakery' pie and pint on the ferry, Magic. We caught the train to Glasgow Central. As usual, I slept most of the journey.
It was then the train back to East Kilbride and into the Monty for a couple of pints, or three, before Irene picked us up at about 10.30pm and took us home.

Craig; *The journey down to Rothesay was uneventful if a bit long. Once there we made up for all the missed refreshment opportunities the tight timetable had created.*
The ferry over to Wemyss Bay gave us the chance to compare draught beer with the canned variety. No contest really but still a worthwhile experiment I think.
Ashore again we found we had time in hand to visit the historical Station Bar.
I am sure that this little bar has seen its fair share of history. Being as it was the jumping off point for decades of

fun filled family holidays, not to mention being the last chance for a nerve calming drink on the way home from a week of unrelenting argument and misery. It has a place in the social history of the working classes of Glasgow. Given the reputation for over indulgence in the West of Scotland I would imagine the Station Bar has also featured more than a few times in district court proceedings. The little bar fairly reeked of character, I'd like to think that's what was reeking anyway.

The rest of the journey home followed the usual format. A quick beer in the Horse Shoe in Glasgow, then an unknown number of beers in the 'Monty' back in East Kilbride. For the sake of accuracy the reason why the number must

Rothesay inner harbour from The Esplanade Hotel

remain unknown is that I tend to reach a tipping point at a certain time of the drinking evening. That is the time where numbers become irrelevant. This leads me to be rubbish at counting beers and also, and more worryingly, crap at Sudoku.

For a project which revels in the title 'The Cheap Way Round' today's epic journey seemed to cost a rather large amount of cash. Notwithstanding necessities such as beer, lets be honest it's only the beer, the cost of this day out was much more than I was expecting.

John; The great thing about this trip was that we had four wee sessions (the Ardrossan to Arran Ferry, Tarbert, Rothesay and the Monty), so although it was quite an expensive day, we had four small hangovers to show for it.

As you can see from the accounts for the day, this is the first trip where food and fares were more than the bevy. We must be slipping, or I have missed counting some of the pints we had.

Spends for the day;

Bus fares	Zero
Train fares	£10.00 approx
Ferry fares	£16.00 approx
Food	£2.00 (pie on ferry)
Drink	£25.00 approx
Total	**£53.00**

Doon the Watter, oan the Batter

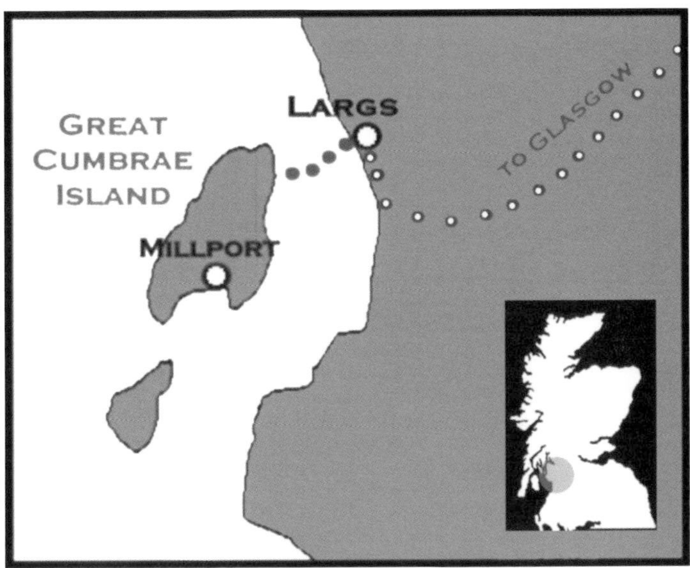

East Kilbride-Glasgow-Largs-Millport
Largs-Glasgow-East Kilbride
(Two Buses, Two Ferries, Four Trains)

John; This was our first trip of the year, and our first ever winter trip. We did the trip in February some time, and from the first picture, you can see there was snow lying. But the forecast was good so we set off. Craig's Irene gave us a lift to EK station, what a woman. We got the 9.48am train into Glasgow, a great deal at only 80p return. If you have to pay for the train, 80p is a good deal.
Craig had planned this trip, which was not much more than a pub crawl in Millport, one of Irene and Craig's favourite places. The original idea was that when we got to Glasgow, we would get the bus for nothing to Largs, a journey of

about one and a half hours, but free. However as we settled into the warm half hour train journey to Glasgow, I suggested that as it would not be too comfortable for Craig to be bounced around on a bumpy McGill's bus for 1.5 hours, did he want to get a return train journey to Largs instead. The extra cost would be less than the price of a pint. Craig eventually agreed (after 30 seconds), so after a pleasant train journey through the snow, we got return tickets to Largs. We wandered round the WH Smiths in the Central Station thinking of something nice to get to eat for the train, but the problem is that there are so many different things, we couldn't make up our minds, so bought nothing, although I bought a medium 'Americana' coffee. This is modern speak for a black coffee. The problem with carry out black coffee is that it burns your hands and takes forever to cool down. We were halfway to Largs before I could enjoy a sip. And the amount of coffee you get is amazing, god knows what size a large one is, Kate says she has never seen one!

It was a lovely run down to Largs. We have done the journey from Largs to Glasgow at the end of a trip, but this was the first time we have gone this way, been sober and awake. We had lovely views of Arran, covered in I snow, and some shitty views of Paisley, Johnston and Kilwinning. As I have said before, you don't want to break down at any of these places.

After checking the times of returning trains, knowing we would never remember, we walked down the main street to the ferry terminal just in time to see the ferry departing. We knew the times between ferries was roughly a pint, so after buying our tickets, we popped over and into *'Charlie Smiths'*, our first pub of the day. It was a very nice pub and we had the usual round, a pint of Lager for Craig, and a pint of Best for me.

Things are looking grim to start

I had assured Craig that we would not have to worry about missing the next ferry as I would see it arriving from my seat at the bar. At about the time when we thought the ferry should have arrived, I realized that my view out the window was not where I thought it was. So we downed our pints and dived across the road, no easy feat for us what with Craig's arthritis and my bad hip. We just got on in time and enjoyed a lovely 10 minute sail over to 'The Great Cumbrae' (Millport is the only town on the island, thought I'd be a smart arse). This was the first time I had been on this ferry without a car and was surprised to find the ferry had a great lounge high up which gave great views all round. Also had good toilet facilities, but no bar, however it was only a 10 minute sail. I couldn't see the point of Calmac building a great lounge high above the deck. By the time you had climbed up the 200 or so stairs, it was time to come down.

Craig smiling at Largs station-2 mins from first pint

On arrival, we walked up the slip and onto the local bus to take us the 10 minute journey into Millport. This was the only journey of the day that was free, apart from the bus back to the slip.

Craig; *Our latest adventure was meant to be a smaller scale version of one of our usual trips. This time our destination was the picturesque town of Millport on the island of Great Cumbrae. As it turned out it was heavy going. That was mainly due to the proximity of the 5 pubs in the town, not to mention a rather good watering hole in Largs. The motivation for the journey was quite simple, I had a sore back and we both fancied a few beers. Another factor to be considered was the weather. We were having quite a lot of weather at the time. Early February is rarely a great time to be travelling round Scotland and the six inches of snow which fell overnight sort of proved that to be a rule.*

The conditions alone would be enough to put off the hardiest of travellers. Obviously that never occurred to us. I put it down to the lure of the booze.
We were determined to get another journey in even though the weather was against us. The reason for that being we had cancelled a much more ambitious trip to the East coast the week before.
Unfortunately I had done something terrible to my back and couldn't manage all that jumping on and off buses. Even a week later I was still in more pain than the average man can tolerate but, as they say, the show must go on. A lesser man would have given in to the pain, but my devotion to duty and of course to Tennent's drove me on. to Largs Usually we would have taken the bus via Gourock but John very graciously suggested that we should go by train to save my back.. We bought our tickets for the ferry as soon as we arrived in Largs and then made straight for the nearest pub for a planning meeting.

John's lookout post

John's strategy of sitting in a seat with a clear view of the ferry terminal was somewhat flawed by his choice of a seat with a panoramic view of a block of flats. God knows how many ferries we missed before we clocked that little faux pas. Still it was a very nice wee pub.
The passengers were boarding by the time we wandered round to the slip. It takes less than ten minutes to cross over to the island and it passed without incident. It could have been really rough. John gets very nostalgic as soon as he gets within sniffing distance of the sea. He likes to remind me that he holds a day skippers' ticket and has seen the full horrors of the sea when he once hired a cabin cruiser. The sea is in his blood apparently.
The bus from the slip dropped us off right outside the George Hotel and after a few minutes trying to decide if the place was open for business we entered.
We were the only customers. In the past I have spent many a good session in the George, but usually that would have been during a busy and noisy weekend.
At one o'clock on a Wednesday in February the atmosphere was rather different. Apart from the two women who were working in the bar the only other person in the place was a hyperactive wean. There are two things in this world I detest. You may have guessed that these things are bad beer and noisy kids. It is fortunate that I never got into a position of power because there would have been big changes to the pub trade. I'm getting a bit worried that John's influence is beginning to have an effect on me.
After a quick and not particularly good pint we moved the twenty or so yards (not metres) to our next venue. Fraser's looks like a good old fashioned Scottish pub. Strangely John had mentioned he didn't like this pub, but I think he changed

his mind during our visit.
The beer was much better and there was a much livelier atmosphere. We even managed to talk to some of the locals. I would have liked to have stayed for another pint or two but we were on a tight timetable.
John; Craig's plan for the day in Millport was to have at least one pint in all five of the bars in the town, so we got off the bus at the terminal at the old pier, and after 30 seconds enjoying the scenic grandeur, we went into the *'Royal George'* which is the only hotel in the town. The bar was like a bar in your living room. The people who own it have spent a bit of money doing the place up, which is a great thing for the town, but the bar area lacks atmosphere and I think I got the first pint of the day, cause it was pretty crap. I drank it anyway. The barmaid's wee girl was running about mad. She told us she was off school as she was not well. In my day if you could walk, you went to school (first rant of the day).
Craig's Irene just loves Millport and was mad Craig wouldn't let her come with us, so Craig kept sending her texts telling how great the weather was, just to annoy her.
We finished our pints and walked the 200 yards or so to the next pub. The walk helped us build up a thirst for our next pint in '*Fraser's Bar'*.
I am happy to say that this was a very nice bar and the pints were great. I explained to the barman about our 'cheap way round' book, I think he thought we were a couple of mad old men.
After the excellent pints and general banter, we bade farewell to '*Fraser's'* and walked the 200 yards to our next pub, which is called '*The Kelburn Bar'*.
We got a fright when I couldn't get the door opened, we thought for a moment that the pub had shut, but after some

complicated door handle turning that would have made a Mason proud, we were in.
Like the other pubs before it, the Kelburn was very quiet. It makes you feel like an alki to be in the pub by yourself,

'Beware: hyperactive weans'

(although Craig was with me, then again I sometimes think he is a bit of an alki.)
The girl behind the bar was good company and told us about her time at college studying history and politics, I think.
We had a couple of good pints and a laugh before we finished and headed the 200 yards to *'The Newton'*.
The Newton is one of the 'line dancing' pubs. It is great during the Country and Western weekend in Millport.
Everybody dresses up in Cowboy gear and wears guns. Come to think of it, a normal weekend in Millport.
We had another excellent pint. By this time we were beginning to enjoy ourselves, the way you can, just before

'Fraser's Bar, our second in Millport

you are too drunk to remember. We said goodbye to '*The Newton'* and walked the 200 yards to *'The Tavern',* or '*Bobby's*', as it is known locally.

This pub is the normal haunt for Craig and Irene when they are in Millport, which is usually about five or six times a year.

Bobby is the name of the owner, he is an old guy, older that me, I think, and is always in the bar. He is a great character and it is a great bar, if you don't mind westerns on the telly all the time. There is sometimes hint of smoke in the bar, which I'm sure comes from the gunshots in the westerns on the telly. Bobby also enjoys a wee refreshment with his customers sometimes, a great barman. I like him.

I had two pints in *Bobby's*, Craig had two and a half, he was starting to speed up, as he does, before we said goodbye to Bobby and got the bus back to the ferry slip.

Hanging on at The Newton, our fourth pub in Millport

The ferry was waiting, and it was with a heavy heart, but lighter wallet, that we got on the ferry and enjoyed the 10 minute sail back across to Largs.

The scenery all around Millport was lovely, everywhere was covered in snow, except an area around the Hunterston Nuclear power station which was lovely and green. Should it have been? Bit of a worry there.

Craig; *The Kelburne is just a few steps along the road and like the other pubs in Millport is quite old fashioned. Once again the beer was quite acceptable. The barmaid was very pleasant and quite talkative. We had an in depth conversation about the pros and cons of island life. To be honest it's a major topic in most of the island's pubs, based on discussions during my many years of enforced holidaying there. Our host's conclusion on island life, if my memory serves me correctly, seemed to be that living in Millport was great then it was rubbish then it was great again. She*

explained that it was a wonderful place to be a child, not so good as a job seeking adult and just a wonderful place to retire to.
It would have been nice to stay a while longer but we were men on a mission. The Newton Bar was not very busy but the beer was good, which after all is the single biggest factor in my enjoyment of any licensed premises. There was only one other customer when we entered , although he could well have been a member of staff. It's never quite clear who's who in Millport. So many of the population have more than one job that you could meet the same person selling you a newspaper in the morning, sorting your washing machine in the afternoon and pouring you your beer in the pub at night.
It was when we went out of the Newton that I took my award winning picture of snow-capped Arran. (see below)
So far we had limited ourselves to a single pint in each pub we had visited as our itinerary was very tight. However the Tavern was next on our list. One of the more unusual features of the Tavern is its' large front window set-up. The glass in the window has a mirrored surface on the outside. This cuts down the suns' glare in the bar, but it also produces hours of harmless fun for the bar-flies inside.

Scenic grandeur-Arran from Millport-Magic

On busy days, unsuspecting tourists use the window mirror to adjust their clothing, hairstyles and, or, makeup. It's better than watching 'you've been framed'. The Tavern is a place I have spent a lot of time in over the last 10 years and therefore deserved a lengthier visit. The proprietor, Bobby, was as usual sitting at the bar watching the telly. Channel 5 if I'm not mistaken. Millport has terrible television reception and Bobby's pub is one of the few places in the town where you can watch that channel. It's a shame really because they do seem to broadcast a lot of westerns, a personal favourite of mine, and more to the point, Bobby's. Two, possibly three pints later and we were out on the street waiting for our bus back round to the slip.

Back in Largs we returned to the bar we had been in earlier for a debriefing sort of a thing.

Officially the journey time from Largs to Glasgow is about an hour. To my recollection it took us about about twenty minutes. Refreshed and ready to resume our tour we

Home from home in 'Bobby's Tavern

hurried to the Horse Shoe Bar for a bit of an après stroll thirst quencher.

John; We arrived back in Largs about 4.45pm, and as the train was leaving at 5.30pm (how we remembered I don't know) we went back into the pub where it all started, *Smiths.* After another excellent pint, we walked up the hill to the station, stopping for Fish and Chips on the way.

As usual, we slept on the train back to Glasgow, then headed to the Horse Shoe. We did think about being sensible and getting a train back to EK, but only for a second or two.

The long sea journey back to the mainland

We got into the Horse Shoe about 6.30pm and left about 7.30pm, so we must have had two pints, Craig might have had three, I have no idea, but we had a great time.

So it was the 7.42pm train back to EK, a walk to the *Monty* and another couple of pints. This cannot be good for us.

We got a taxi home and I arrived home skint, but happy.

Kate told me in the morning that I had 12 pints, How does she know?. I have since counted up how many pints we did have (roughly) and the answer is 12, although Craig may have had 14. It's a lot of drink and I am not proud of it. I have to say that in case Kate reads this.

Craig; *Our return to East Kilbride, the visit to the 'Monty' and the taxi home all passed without incident, apparently. I was just a little bit tired by this time and much of the detail escapes me. John assures me we had a great time.*

Spends for the day;

Bus fares	£0.00
Train fares	£7.00 approx
Ferry fares	£2.00 approx
Food	£2.50 half a fish supper
Drink	£30.00 approx (includes cup of coffee)
Total	**£41.50**

On the Buses-Off the Bevy

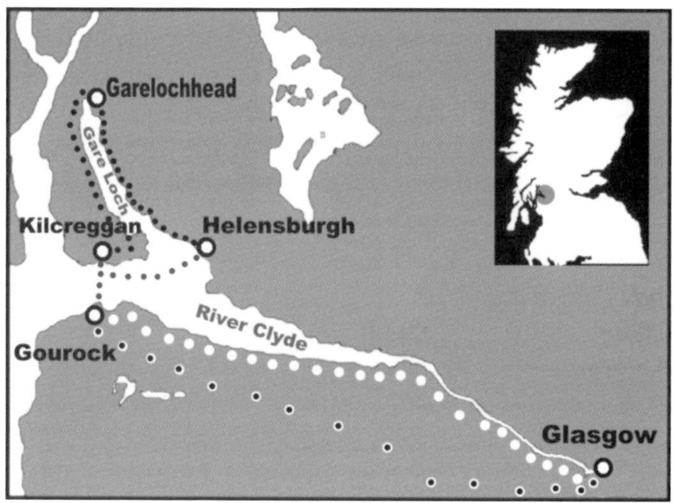

East Kilbride-Glasgow-Gourock-Kilcreggan
Garelochead-Helensburgh-Gourock-Glasgow
(Three Buses-Two Boats-Three Trains)

John; We are back on the road. This is our first trip since my hip operation in the Southern General Hospital. I now have two metal hips. Airports will be a bigger nightmare than normal. Rubber gloves to the fore.

Craig, however, has a real problem. He was rushed into hospital last week and it has transpired that although he has been let out, he has to return in six weeks for an operation to remove a Gall Stone and I think the Bladder as well. That is not the problem. He has been ordered to lay off the bevy and fatty foods. As all we do on our trips, apart from travelling about Scotland, is drinking pints and eating fish suppers, you can see what the problem is going to be.

Leaving EK-sober-we returned the same way

We decided, however, to go ahead with the trip and see what it would be like to remember what happens on a trip.

This is a trip we have been talking about for a while, it takes in an area we have not been to and we take a boat, not a ferry.

This is a small boat that plies between Gourock, Kilcreggan and Helensburgh all day-magic.

Craig; *Our last trip turned out to be more of a beer-fest than a leisurely journey around the West of Scotland. This time things would be very different, and not through choice on my part.*

Due to a serious medical condition, one which would lay low a lesser man, I would be unable to consume any alcohol. It's really quite hard to imagine why anyone would choose to spend their day travelling for miles by train, boat and bus without so much as a sniff of booze. Such was my devotion to the cause that I was willing to endure this hardship.

John; Kate (the luckiest woman in the world), dropped us at

EK station on a lovely sunny, but very windy, morning. The 9.18 train got us into Glasgow Central, giving us plenty of time to walk up to St. Vincent Street to catch the legendry McGill's Glasgow to Largs flier. It turned up almost on time, and was very busy with the silver headed. It was a glorious day and we had a lovely run to Gourock. I sat facing backward on the bus, you get a completely different view going backwards. I liked it very much. Everywhere looks nice on a sunny day, except Port Glasgow and Greenock, which need more than good weather to look reasonable.
We arrived at the pier in plenty time for the boat and watched as it ploughed its way over in very wild conditions.
We actually wondered if the conditions would lead to the sailing being cancelled, but all was ok, and we boarded for the 11.35 sailing to Kilcreggan. Craig was checking out the boarding facilities for a future bike trip, but the gang-plank was very narrow, and even in calm conditions Craig did not think he could get his bike onboard. I offered to come down to help, but he knew I would only laugh at his attempt.

Our wee boat makes heavy weather of the crossing

So the wee boat ploughed through heavy seas to Kilcreggan. I stayed on deck, being an experienced sailor, but Craig stayed inside, what a nancy, although he was popping a lot of painkillers. I asked if he was in a lot of pain, but he assured me it was to kill the pain of listening to my ranting without a drink inside him.

Craig; *The trip down to Gourock was a bit bumpy but otherwise uneventful. Thankfully we didn't have much time to kill so there was no chance of being tempted to indulge in a little refreshment before we caught the wee boat across to Kilcreggan.*

The wind was getting up a bit so the trip over was a bit rougher than we expected. Fortunately we are both good sailors so there were no embarrassing mishaps.

Arriving at Kilcreggan Pier

Kilcreggan looks like a nice little place and I'm sure it is. I just didn't get to see it at its best. That is to say I was stone cold sober and likely to remain so. Trust me, a few beers can make even the dreariest shanty town look 'no bad '.

John; We disembarked (got off) the boat and wandered slowly up the pier into the sleepy hamlet of Kilcreggan.

There was no hurry because we were not looking for a pub. After a walk along the main street (200 yards), we found a café-bar type place with two tables outside. The café was on the corner of "Temperance Brae" which was apt as Craig was off the bevy. Craig had a cup of tea and I had a coffee (what are friends for). If there is a plus side, it was a glorious day and we were looking over the Firth of Clyde

Craig; *We had half an hour to wait for our bus up to Garelochhead and usually this would be our cue to leg it to the nearest boozer for a swift pint. Not this time. It might take years to live it down but we ended up at a small café sipping tea. As I sat there with teacup in hand I felt really strange. I could imagine generations of Stevensons past, spinning in their graves at the sight of me sitting there slurping down that lukewarm brew.*

After our tea we made our way to the bus stop where we got into conversation with a chap who had been on the boat with us. We were talking about the strangely named Temperance Brae which was right beside the bus stop when a local woman stopped to tell us the history behind it's name. It appears that the hotel just along from the Brae had been a temperance hotel before it closed down a few years ago.

Apparently the locals are not what you would call overly imaginative when it comes to naming things.

Two things occurred to me at this point. I don't think anyone would be stunned to learn that a temperance hotel failed to capture enough trade to be viable in Scotland. Secondly, John forgoing his usual pint of 70/- to show solidarity with my plight wasn't really making much of a sacrifice when you realise there wasn't actually a pub in the place. By now it was beginning to look like neither of us was meant to get anywhere near a pub that day.

John; Our non-alcoholic drinks finished, we wandered along to the bus stop to catch the 12.19pm bus number 316, pretty good detailed information. Amazing what you remember without bevy involved.

The photo above says it all

The bus was to take us up to the village of Garelochhead. Wonder where they got the name from.

It was a lovely run with great scenery. The only blot on the landscape was the view over to Faslane where the navy keeps all its Nuclear Submarines and other secret things. It was the first time I had seen Faslane from this side of the loch, it is massive. The number of accommodation buildings makes the place look like Castlemilk.

We got off the bus and had a walk through the village, which looked very nice, although in glorious sunshine almost everywhere looks nice.

Although he was off the bevy, Craig insisted we go into the local pub so I could have a pint. So we entered '*The Anchor*

Inn', which is the only pub in the village. The place was packed and it only took us a couple of minutes to realize that it was a funeral party. The black ties and suits gave it away. Anyway, it must have been an old and expected passing as everyone, except sober Craig and me, were enjoying themselves.
So I ordered a pint of Best, and Craig had a problem. Being a true bevy merchant, I don't think he had ever ordered a soft drink, so was unsure what to do. Eventually he opted for a pint of diluting orange with lemonade. It looked, and probably tasted like piss. After finishing our pints, I insisted that I didn't want another (what a friend I am). So we went outside and across the road and sat in the sunshine eating our pieces. It was a lovely view across the loch and we enjoyed the solemnity and sobriety, of the moment.
It was getting near our bus time so we wandered over to the bus stop. While waiting for the bus, we were approached by a couple of Jakies carrying fishing rods who said they had been fishing. I feigned surprise. One of them, who was stripped to the waist asked me, and I quote, "when are the Mackerel coming back". I replied that I didn't know they had gone. A vacant look followed.
Craig; *The weather had fairly brightened up by the time we caught the bus for Garelochhead. It was a very pleasant journey with great views of the loch.*
Garelochhead is very small with only a handful of quiet roads. The main street runs along the loch shore and after a very short walk along it we decided to check out the pub. The Anchor Inn is a traditional country pub. It is well laid out, quite spacious with lots of wood panelling and brass.
As you can imagine it took all my powers of persuasion to get John to take a real drink. He celebrated by telling everyone who would listen to him that I was teetotal and

Craig's' pint of what looks like piss being poured

reduced to drinking orange juice and lemonade. This seemed to keep him amused for a good twenty minutes.

In what must feature as a major, and infrequent, event in my drinking career I finished my first pint and, without ordering another, left the pub.

Waiting for the bus to Helensburgh we got into conversation with two of life's more challenged wee souls. I really should have taken a photograph of them as they looked like a couple of extras from the film 'Trainspotting'. The one who could speak, as opposed to the one who just grunted, told us they had been fishing there for a couple of days. They had so far caught nothing at all. This didn't surprise me one little bit. To be honest I doubt they were ever likely to catch anything. In a battle of wits my money would be on the fish.

The chatty one was stripped to the waist and had the beginnings of a good lobster tan. His 'jakey' pal, by contrast, looked like he had dressed for a nights dossing in

Après piece at Garelochhead

shop doorways. Baggy trousers and long hooded jackets seem to the uniform of the socially inadequate. Maybe he would fit in with the soap dodgers down the road at Faslane. Passing the 'Peace Camp' was the only highlight of the bus trip down to Helensburgh. I managed to catch a glimpse of the shy creatures who inhabit this ramshackle collection of tents and caravans. The peace campaigners seemed to be having a day off from whatever it is they do. Assuming they actually do anything. The place is a complete eyesore but it has been allowed to stay there for years. If it had been a couple of travelling families the police would have been right in there with truncheons blazing after a few days. But that's politics for you. I'm now getting worried that I'm turning into a clone of John.

John; We got on the bus with the Jakies and had a nice run down the other side of the loch to Helensburgh, on the way passing the camp with the protesters. It looked deserted to us, so it looks like it was too warm a day for protesting.

We had a wander along the front of Helensburgh and found

a pub. This time I talked Craig into a pint of fresh orange and lemonade. He admitted this tasted much better, but a long way off a pint of lager.

We walked to the pier and saw the two jakies trying to catch something, with no luck. They should be at work rather than messing about spending their broo money on fishing rods and talking through their one nostril.

We watched the wee boat come over from Gourock in very windy and rough conditions. The return sail was to Kilcreggan and then Gourock, so it was a fairly long sail in massive seas. As I am a born sailor, it was no problem for me, but I was expecting Craigs' Orange Juice all over the boat at one point.

Craig wondering what a beer would taste like right now

Craig; *Helensburgh looks like any other West of Scotland seaside town. That is to say, 30 years behind the times and dying on its feet. After a quick wander up and down the front*

I decided that it was time to let John have another infusion of alcohol. I had another orange juice, just to keep him amused.
The Station Bar is a rather old fashioned little place. Normally I would have liked that about the place but, things were far from normal. That's the thing about orange juice, it keeps you both sober and regular.
Down on the pier we saw our two jakey friends from earlier. Still fishless. You would think that given the size of the Clyde Estuary and the fish conservation strategies of the EU in the last decade or so they could hardly fail to catch at least one fish.
John; After a great sail, during which Craig proved he was a real man of the sea, with no fear, at least none I could smell, we arrived safely back in Gourock after a very enjoyable day on the Cowal district, and got on the train, sober for the first time, to take us back to Glasgow Central Station.
Craig; *We enjoyed the boat trip back to Gourock and got into the station with plenty of time to catch our train to Glasgow. However, John had other ideas apparently. Being unable to find to find the toilets on the train he wandered off to find one at the ferry port.*
As the time ticked bye and John had not returned my blood pressure nudged towards the hypertensive zone. He eventually sauntered round the corner just as the guard was about to blow his whistle. I hate cliff-hangers, especially when I haven't had the benefit of a few nerve calming beers.
The homeward trip was uneventful. I didn't even manage my usual power nap.
John; We then, for the first time ever, did not go to the Horseshoe Bar, but got on the first train to EK, where Kate, the present Mrs. Mackay, was waiting to run us home. Even without the bevy, or only two pints in my case, we had a

great day, but hope Craig will be better for the next adventure.

Craig; *This latest journey had proved very different from all that had gone before. The main difference as far as I'm concerned is the fact that I can remember all of it. Some people might say that having a clear memory is a good thing. Not me. The total lack of booze in the system means that I can't really exaggerate, invent or lie about what we got up to. This is a major draw-back to us as our writing depends on the artistic license provided by a moderate intake of booze. Much of what we write about is pub based or at least inspired by the many hours we spend there, talking to locals and bar professionals. If you remove the pub from the equation what's left could be a very short travelogue.*

The one saving grace of this trip was that for once it really was the cheap way round.

John; This trip was, by far, our cheapest trip to date, and no doubt will be the cheapest trip ever. No drink and no fish suppers, we are now the healthiest two drunks in EK.

Trips financial details;

Bus fares	£0.00
Train fares	£4.00 approx
Boat fares	£4.80
Food	£0.00
Drink	£4.60 (two pints)
Total	**£13.40**

Nae Fees on the High Seas

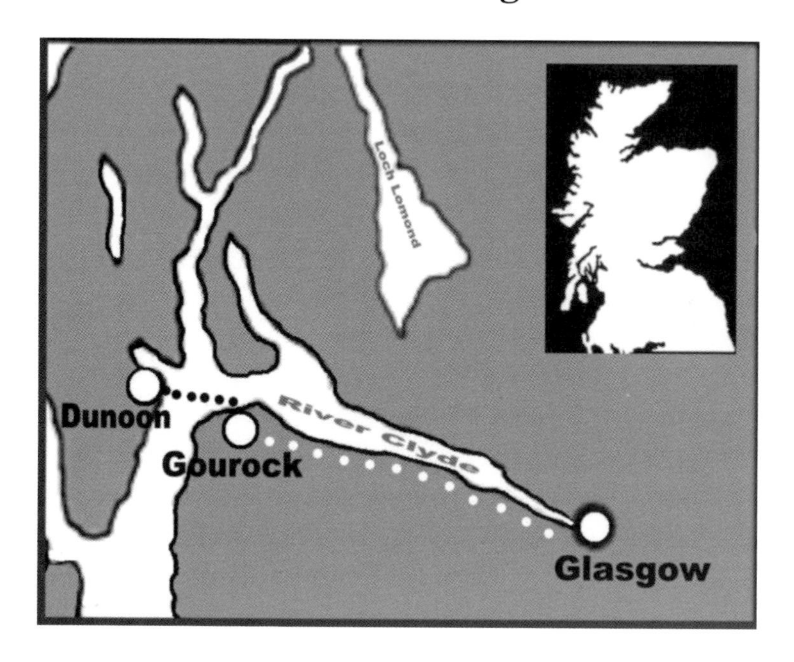

East Kilbride-Glasgow-Dunoon-Glasgow-East Kilbride
(Two Buses, Two Trains, Two Ferries)

John; This was a very short, but ground breaking trip. Craig is still waiting to go into hospital for his operation, but is feeling well, and looking great as he has not had a drink, or any fatty food for 19 weeks! What a bore. We just decided the day before to go on this short trip. The ground breaking part for us is that we can go on two ferries for nothing. A lifelong ambition achieved.
How it works is that McGill's, the coach company of mixed performance, lay on a coach from Buchanan Street to Dunoon, via Western Ferries from Gourock

Kate waving us off on our free trip to Dunoon

The bus goes on the ferry and you don't have to pay, if you are an oldie. I don't know what the youngsters pay, and am not likely to find out as our coach, holding over 60 people, all over 60 years of age, did not take in a penny. But more of that later.

Kate, the often mentioned, but never photographed, luckiest lady in the world waved me off on a glorious Friday (I think) morning. I walked down to Irene and Craig's where Irene was ready to drive us down to EK train station.

Irene dropped us off at the station in time to catch the 9.18am to Central Station. Little did we know on the way into Glasgow that the return journey would provide one of the dramatic train journey events of our adventures to date, more of that later also.

Craig; *Our trip to Dunoon was definitely a spur of the moment sort of thing. Usually that means that we have been overdoing it down at the Crooked Lum. Not so this time.*

John had heard of this bus trip which would take us all the way to Dunoon, ferry crossing included. To be honest I don't think either of us initially believed that such a service existed. Being wrong is nothing new to us but, this time at least, we were happy to be so. It is the dream of the money conscious traveller everywhere; a free sail on a ferry. I've lost count of the number of schemes John has come up with to get a free hurl on a boat.

We have both tried, unsuccessfully, to work out how McGill's can make any money on this service. The best I could come up with was that someone had made a huge accounting error and sooner or later it would be found out.

Another reason for our trip was down to frustration. We had missed out on our regular jaunts around Scotland for most of the summer because of my malfunctioning gall bladder. It was proving to be a bit more complicated than first thought. I'd been in hospital having some unspeakable procedures inflicted on me. The upshot was that instead of a six week wait for an operation I would have to hang on for five months. John, par for the course, had little sympathy for me, suggesting that I was just 'acting it'. To keep him from moaning I agreed to this short trip.

John; We arrived at Central Station, as we always do and walked out into the great city of Glasgow, '*The Second City'*, the sun was shining and the other oldies awaited us.

We were concerned that the typical McGill's coach, which is fairly small with a low, very bumpy floor would be very busy as it was a lovely day and the idea of a free trip, including ferry journey would be too much for most oldies to ignore . So we hurried up to the bus station and arrived there about 20 minutes before departure time.

There were two rows of seats for people to await the arrival of the coach and we took our place on two of the seats, other people moved up. Most people, but not all, know how to queue.

At about five minutes before departure, about five oldies just walked up to the front, kidding on the sun was in their eyes, and stood at the front so they would be first on the coach, you could have cut the atmosphere with a knife. I think we must be cross breeding with the Italians too much. These bastards have no idea on how to queue, but more of that on another rant.

As soon as the bus was seen in the distance, there was a rush to get to the front of the queue. The speed at which old people move over a short distance is exceptional. However, it was a big coach and we were near the front, so we got a great seat near the back at the emergency exit. I thought this was a great idea as we were going to be sitting on the bus while it was on the ferry.

There was always a possibility that the Waverley might be

Craig looks forward to another half gallon of orange juice

passing and the captain might have his mind on other things, as has happened in the past. You only have to mention the "Gantocks", and he is on them.

The bus was completely full, and I reckon Craig was by far the youngest person on the bus.

I am certain that this trip by McGill's only operates because of the Government giving us oldies free travel. They must be bunging Western Ferries something for each passenger, so there must be plenty of profit to be made from the government.

The magnificent Glasgow Central Station

One of my earliest rants about how the Scottish Parliament could not afford to give us all free bus travel has been proven correct. There has been a lot of talk in the newspapers recently about it all costing to much money. They really are a shower of numpties!

The caption on the photo below sums up the people who travel all over Scotland for free, us. God bless the numpties. It was another glorious day and we enjoyed the run down to Gourock passing all the places we had passed before. But in the sunshine, the Clyde estuary is always beautiful (except Port Glasgow and Greenock, as usual).

A quote from Craig, 'The grey hair and the nae hair

At the stop before the ferry terminal, an oldie got on the bus and after not paying, got a free trip on the ferry-magic.

Craig; *Buchannan Bus Station is not my favourite place to be first thing in the morning. This free travel malarkey has made things worse recently. Now there are gangs of the grey haired roaming the concourse cluttering up the place.*

There is a famous statue in the main hall of the station. It shows a young couple greeting each other with a passionate embrace. Given the recent changes perhaps it could be replaced by a statue of a couple of old codgers complaining at the enquiry desk.

This time round we decided not to give the old buggers to much leeway when it came to getting on the bus. On our first trip from this station we naively believed that the silver generation would behave with dignity and respect when it came to queuing for the bus. Fat chance. They were like rabid dogs. McGill's service from Glasgow to Dunoon always looked like being a codger only affair. As we waited at the stance for the bus, I could see gangs of them circling our position. They were fooling no one. Certainly not us anyway. We held our nerve and forced our way on to the bus.

The trip down to Gourock was uneventful. We've travelled it so often in the last year or so that I didn't even bother looking out of the window. Come to think of it there's not a lot worth looking out at.

John; The journey over was very warm as the bus was sitting in the sun with the doors shut. Also the ferry was very slow and we had virtually no view because of the position of the bus on the ferry. We felt it would be ungrateful to complain as it was all free.

The bus eventually drove off the ferry and in about five minutes we got off the bus at the terminal in Dunoon opposite the pier and also opposite a great pub called 'The View', (a pub we have visited on previous trips when Craig was bevying). However, it is not his fault he is no well, so I never dig him up about it (Aye, right).

We wandered down onto the pier as Craig wanted some photographs of the very nice buildings on the pier. The buildings are unique to Dunoon and, as you can see from the photograph on the next page, are very unusual.

After we had taken our photographs, we wandered along to a small café on the front, with seats outside, and had our lunch. Craig felt a bit embarrassed as he had pieces, but we ordered other stuff to eat and drink and Craig sneaked his pieces up from under the table. As we were about the only

The delightful building on Dunoon pier

people sitting outside, nobody would have given a toss what we were doing.

As you can see from the photo opposite, it was a lovely place to have our lunch, even without a bevy.

We didn't have long in Dunoon as I had to be back in EK by about five as Kate and I were going out. So we had a wander along the front in the sunshine and got on the coach, which appeared out of nowhere when I was away wandering.

Craig; *It was a very sunny day by this time and I wondered how the oldies would stand up to the rising temperature. I had a sneaking suspicion that there might be a number of empty seats on the way back to Glasgow. Things didn't improve at the ferry port as we had to wait quite a while for the boat to come in.*

I have heard that using the air-conditioning in your car uses quite a bit of fuel. Presumably the same is true with buses. That would explain why it was so hot on our coach. Perhaps switching on the air-conditioning would bugger up the profit margins.

On our sail over to Hunter's Quay we had an outstanding view of the side of the boat. Fifteen minutes of staring at a blank wall did nothing to improve my mood. Knowing that I couldn't even have a beer when we eventually got off the ferry didn't help much either.

For the second consecutive trip I found myself sitting drinking tea at a seaside café. It's enough to make you greet. The one compensation was the views of the Firth of Clyde were fantastic.

We finished our tea then strolled back along towards the quay. John decided to treat himself to a cone. I thought it was a poor substitute for a beer so declined to join him.

John; The bus had a better position on the ferry on the way back over to Gourock and we had a nice view.

On the way back into Glasgow, we managed to get off the bus at the end of Bothwell Street, right next to the Central Station which saved us about half an hour. In the old days this would have meant two extra pints, but now it meant we got the earlier train home, pathetic.

This meant, however, that we witnessed a dramatic happening at Clarkston Station when an old man dropped his mobile phone onto the line and jumped down after it. At least we think this is what happened. The result was that the old guy and a young girl ended up running up the line to the end of the platform as he was too old to climb back up onto it. Our train was in an uproar-everybody was talking to everybody else-just like the old days. Anyway, the old bloke survived and we all got back to nobody talking to each other for the rest of the trip, except Craig and me.

Kate, bless her, picked us up from EK station and our quick and sober trip was over.

Craig enjoying his illegal piece

I'm not going into details of the cost of the trip as it was almost nothing. The sooner Craig gets back on the bevy the better.

Craig; *The only highlight of our journey home was when a nutter jumped onto the railway line. I thought it was a very clumsy suicide attempt as there wasn't actually a train coming. Perhaps it was just a dry run for a future go at it. By he look of the old guy who jumped onto the line he could save himself a lot of hassle if he just let time take it's course. After that excitement it was home in time for yet another cup of tea.*

This little journey of ours could well go down as the most successful trip we have, or are ever likely to plan. It completely fulfils our objective of travelling on the cheap. If we had taken a flask of tea with us instead of going to that wee café it would have been completely free.

The Western ferry heads East to Gourock

It's a cruel irony that on a trip where hee haw happened an alcohol ban meant I could remember every bit of it. Life is just not fair. Still there's always my operation to look forward to.

Costs for the day; **Nothing**

Bevy Merchant Returns

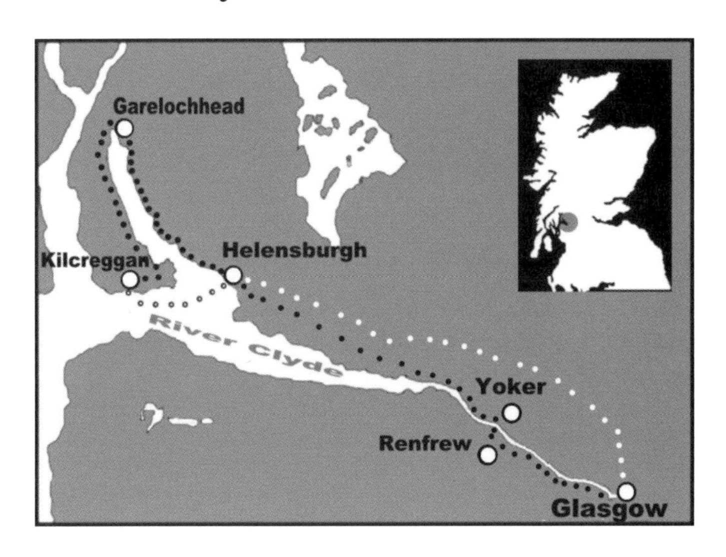

EastKilbride-Glasgow-Renfrew-Yoker-Helensburgh-Kilcreggan-Garelochhead-Helensburgh-Glasgow-East Kilbride
*(*Four Buses,ThreeTrains, Two Ferries)

John; This was our first full trip with Craig back to full health and strength and back on the bevy (only Glasgow people would be happy about that). It was also an historic trip because the main reason for it was to cross the legendary 'Renfrew Ferry' before the council close it down at the end of this month (February). It is either close it down or take away our free bus passes. Who needs the ferry anyway?
Craig; *We don't often need much of an excuse to take off on one of our little excursions. A bit of scenery and the*

prospect of a beer or two is usually enough to get us on the road. This journey was different. This trip was important for historical and social reasons. I would like to say that we spent hours researching our subject, but there's no way I could make that sound believable. To be honest the planning was what might be called haphazard.

We had read in the papers, or perhaps it was on the telly, that one of Scotland's oldest institutions was to be scrapped. The Renfrew Ferry was to be stopped. We were outraged. Something had to be done. Eventually we decided that we should show our support for the ferry by including it in one of our travels. While we were ranting on about history and tradition I realized that I'd never actually been on the ferry or even knew where Renfrew or Yoker were. Time to put that right.

The Renfrew Ferry has been travelling back and forth between Renfrew and Yoker on the Clyde for over 500 years. Presumably there have been several different ferries since the service began. Although the old guy taking the tickets looked like he might have been around for a good few years of the service.

Since we would be quite close to an area we had visited before it was decided that there were two or three pubs which deserved a second chance to impress us. This time round we intended to actually have a beer in them.

John; So it was with heavy heart, and a heavy wallet (I reckon we would visit eight pubs) that we set off on a fine Monday morning. Kate drove us down to the EK train station to catch the 9.29am, the first train I could get for the cheap 80p return.

We arrived in Glasgow Central, wandered across Renfield Street and caught McGill's old X23 to take us to Renfrew.

The bus was an earlier one than I'd planned so we arrived

in Renfrew about 10.30am, half an hour before the pubs open. I knew Renfrew well, as I used to thumb a lift to the baths there from Linthouse some Saturdaymornings when I was young.

Ye olde Renfrew Ferry

Later, when I was old enough, I used to drink in the Ferry Inn now and again

Craig; *We arrived at the ferry well before 11am and found the place busy with a constant stream of middle aged men carrying cameras pacing up and down the slipway. These failed train spotters were almost falling over each other frantically searching for something to photograph. I thought it was quite sad actually, then I realized we fitted right in. That made it tragic.*

Everyone was asking if we'd seen the new aqua bus which was supposed to be undergoing tests there. Being old hands

at this investigation lark we knew the answers to all our questions lay behind the doors of the Ferry Inn. So we went in. Two pints of inspiration later and we knew where the bus was and what it had been up to. Barmen always know what's going on. The bus was parked behind the pub.
It seems a bit odd to me that the manufacturer of an amphibious vehicle would have it painted bright yellow. It might well be highly visible, but you can't help thinking 'Yellow Submarine'. Not too reassuring for the slightly nervous traveller. It's a bit like naming the new Millport Ferry 'The MV Titanic'.
John; So we wandered down the road to the ferry and found there were quite a few people hanging about. We assumed at first that they, like us, were waiting for 'The Ferry Inn to open, but this was not the case. Some of them had cameras with tripods and everything. They were waiting for the arrival of a new bus/boat which had been featured in the Scottish news recently.

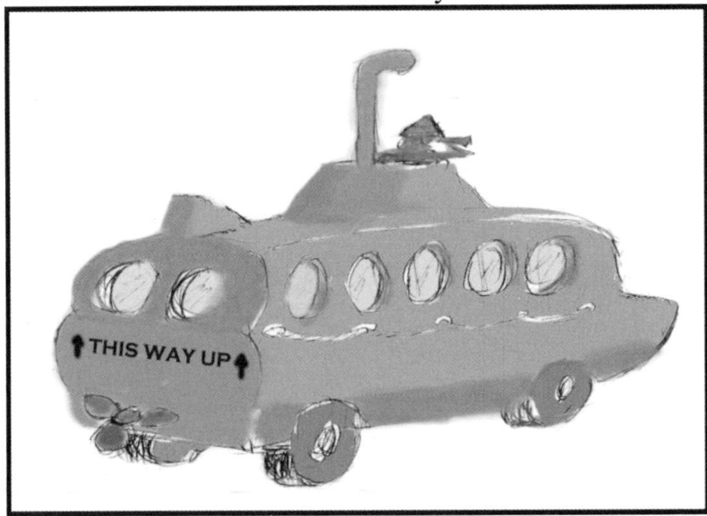

Bus, boat or submarine

This bus is being tested with a view to driving right across the river with people in it. This is no kidding. Sounds like a floating coffin to me. Mind you, if it sinks, it will be all oldies who drown, what a way to go.
As finding this information, and taking some pictures of the Ferry, took us to 11.00am, we went right into the Ferry Inn for a couple of pints. This was a very poignant moment as it was Craig's first pint back on the road. The Inn was very nice, as old men's pubs go. As normal on our trips, we were the first people in. The smell of bleach was overpowering, but I suppose it means it's clean, unless pubs just spill a wee drop every morning to give the effect of being cleaned.
We found out after talking to the barman that the bus/boat was just parked behind the Inn, so after a couple of enjoyable pints, we sneaked around the back and took a photo of this big yellow bus with what looked like propellers at the back. This thing has been developed in Holland, which is apt as I reckon they should supply a little Dutch boy with each bus/boat in case there is a leak. Will have to check if us oldies get on the floating coffin for nothing.
We wandered down to the ferry and there was a sign telling us that although the fare was £1.20, us oldies got on for nothing-magic. The trip took about two minutes, but while we were on the ferry sailing over to Yoker, the big yellow bus came out from behind the 'Ferry Inn', much to the delight of the waiting camera people. Unfortunately for them, it turned the other way and buggered off without so much as a splash. Craig and I found this hilarious. We'd had two pints remember.
We wandered up to Dumbarton Road to find the bus stop. Our plan was to catch the 204 to Dumbarton and then the

216 from there to Helensburgh. On checking the timetable at the bus shelter, we found that the 216 went from here right to Helensburgh. This would save us about 40 minutes (two pints). So we decided that since Dumbarton is the north shore equivalent of Greenock (a dump), there was a great looking old pub across the road called The Anchorage, and we had 'the Taste', we would take advantage of the one bus option. So after checking when our bus was due, we wandered in and had a very enjoyable couple of pints.

Just to calm the nerves

While supping our drink, we found out that when the school leaving age in Yoker went up from 15 to 16, there was nothing for the kids to do, just like now. So the headmaster got them all to bring in any historical information they could get from their parents and the school wrote a book on the history of Yoker. This was of absolutely no interest to

us, but it passed a happy half hour, and the wee guy who told us the historical information was a nice wee man who needed someone to talk to, a bit like me. The barmaid was very nice, but has had a hell of a time getting to and from work recently with all the snow. It was a great wee pub to relax in after our voyage over the Clyde.
We got on the 216 which arrived right on time and had a nice wee run down to Helensburgh, although you pass through some right rough looking places on the outskirts of Dumbarton. On the bus Craig mentioned that he thought he could smell onions. I could too. The aroma was coming from my pieces which Kate had made for me. They had 'Isle of Bute' Cheddar and chopped up Red Onions, I had smelled the onion before but didn't like to mention it. The reason for the change from my beloved Corn Beef was that this trip was only decided the night before and our larder had no Corned Beef. I did not give Kate a row, I knew she felt bad enough at letting me down in such a big way. Forgive and forget I say. The pieces were delicious, I love cheese and onion (but got to be 'Isle of Bute' cheese). The amazing thing is that Kate had wrapped up the pieces very well in tin foil. You obviously canny keep the smell of onion from escaping. During this bus journey, we both ate our pieces without the driver noticing, although some of the passengers were licking their lips and wiping their eyes.
Craig; *The bus trip to Helensburgh seemed to take forever. I think it stopped every hundred yards or so. There was something strange about the bus and first I couldn't put my finger on just what it was. To call it an odour just didn't cover it. It turned out to be Johns' pieces for the journey. I prefer to call them his sandwiches of mass destruction. He claimed it was just onion but I didn't think so. It was bad enough while they were wrapped, but once they hit the air*

their full force was unleashed. Small children were crying and frantically rubbing their eyes. I was really worried in case the fumes reached the driver. The image of firemen in bio-protective suits picking through the wreckage of the old 216 flitted through my mind.

Luckily for me, and of course the rest of the passengers, John scoffed his pieces at heroic speed and therefore saved everyone from serious injury. God knows where Kate got her hands on weapons grade onions.

John; I was bursting for the toilet by the time we got off the bus in Helensburgh, so we fairly sprinted along the front and into The Clyde Bar. The best thing you can say about the bar is that it sells drink and has lovely views from the door.

We did however find important information from the other man at the bar, and that was that there was a pub open in Kilcreggan, our next port of call. This was important to us as we have been to Kilcreggan before, when Craig was tee total, and there was no pub open, but it did not matter so much then.

So, after a couple of pints, which were not as good as the ones in 'The Anchorage', we walked down the long pier at Helensburgh as our wee boat approached, it was a lovely day, although a wee bit cold.

Craig; *It was great to revisit The Clyde Bar in Helensburgh because this time round I got to savour a couple of brews. The last time it was strictly orange juice.*

John; After a lovely 20 minute sail, we arrived in Kilcreggan. It was a laugh getting off, as Craig couldn't find the tickets and the man was starting to ask him to buy new ones. This was same guy who watched Craig buying the tickets on the way on. He was from Poland, we think, and couldn't speak much English, and as Craig's from

Auchinleck, most English people, let alone Poles, can't understand him. Craig found the tickets eventually, which stopped the wee Pole from being vaulted into the Clyde.

Craig; *We could see the little ferry coming across to the pier as we left the bar. Once on the ferry I bought the tickets and on the way to the stairs I nodded over to the crewman who was standing watching us. I said something like 'fine day'! but he didn't respond. You get used to that level of personal attention when you travel around Scotland!*

We spent the next ten minutes or so taking pictures of each other pointing at scenery then made our way back up to disembark. That's when the trouble started. My non speaking friend from earlier now decided to get vocal. He stuck out his hand and demanded 'TICKETS'.

I thought the man was just a bit hard of hearing or something. It turned out he was foreign. Needless to say I had misplaced the tickets. I just kept handing him all the little pieces of paper I had in my pocket. I'm pretty sure I managed to hand him a couple of Kit Kat wrappers. Every time I handed him a piece of paper he would utter the same phrase, 'is not a ticket'. Out of the corner of my eye I could see John standing on the pier laughing his head off. By this time it was obvious to me that my eastern European friend knew next to no English. This doesn't seem to be a drawback to a career in Scottish tourism but it was hampering my efforts to get off the boat. I decided to revert to my Ayrshire roots and told him, 'Am no paying twice'. This seemed to do the trick and I was allowed to get ashore.

John; As the boat approached the pier, we could see welcoming lights in what looked like, and turned out to be, a lovely pub called 'The Lighthouse'. So after wandering up the pier, in we went.

East meets West

It was a lovely pub, which an Irish couple have taken over recently. The young lady, Liz was her name, was very nice, and laughed all the time. Even if you said something which wasn't funny, she would burst out laughing. It was great, although I think it would become a bit wearing after a couple of hours. I started to tire of her humour when she told us that when we walked in she thought we were Jack and Victor from 'Still Game'. What a cheek. This comment reminded me of our local barman Russell saying to Kate one day that he always thinks of 'Last of the Summer Wine' when Craig and I walk into his bar in EK. Anyway, if you did not want to listen to the female laughing policeman, there was a lovely view over the Clyde to Gourock from the bar, and I would advise anyone that a sail over to Kilcreggan from Helensburgh, or Gourock, and an hour or so spent in 'The Lighthouse' would be a pleasant way to spend an afternoon.

Craig; *It's only a hundred yards or so from the pier to The Lighthouse and we covered the distance at a fair pace. A sea crossing works wonders for the thirst. On our last visit we were told the hotel had been closed for some time. The Good Samaritan/busybody who stopped to give us this information also told us it had been called The Temperance Hotel, so, as you can imagine, we had no real interest in going there anyway. Things had certainly changed for the better.*
The Lighthouse was not at all what I expected. It was bright and modern and as it turned out, quite lively. The landlady it has to be said was a larger than life character. A character without a volume control. She had a fantastic Irish accent and would make a great Mrs. Doyle if they ever decided to re-make the Father Ted TV series. I'm not just saying that because she compared the two of us to a couple of old codgers from yet another television programme. The cheek of some people.

A couple of comedy look-alikes?

John; We left in time to catch the Bus No. 316 at 4.18pm to Garelochhead. We have, as our avid readers will know, done this part of the journey before, but sober. After a few pints, it is the same, only the scenery is slightly out of focus, and the Submarine base at Faslane still looks terrible.
We got off the bus in Garelochhead and headed straight into 'The Anchor Bar'. We knew from Liz that the girl who ran the bar was called Kathleen, so after introducing ourselves as friends of Liz, and Craig telling her that we were travel writers studying pubs in Scotland, we still were not offered a free pint. I wonder if this happens to Bill Bryson.
The pints were great, as was Kathleen, so even though she is a tight fisted barmaid, it is a great wee pub to visit.
Then it was back out into the dark night and on to the next No.316 to Helensburgh. We could not see much due to the darkness, but this did not matter as we have been on this bus on more sober times.
We wandered around Helensburgh until we found a chip shop and bought fish suppers. They were delicious, although I think they always taste better when you've had a few pints. We ate them on the hoof (walking about) and bought our train tickets. As we still had about half an hour to kill, we wandered across the road from the station into the 'Station Bar', no idea how they worked out that name. It was another old man's bar. The locals did not seem too friendly in this pub so we drank our pint quietly and then headed back across to the station, got on the train and slept most of the journey to Queen Street. Only exciting thing to happen was that Craig fell up the stairs, 'nothing to do with the drink'.
Craig; *While travelling down from Helensburgh it occurred to me that John probably thinks that all trains in Scotland are on a par with the French High Speed trains. As far as*

he is concerned it only ever takes about twenty minutes to travel back from any mainline station in Scotland.
I do have to admit that I am quite jealous of his ability to nod off so easily.
Back in Glasgow we hurried from the train, as time is precious to all serious beer connoisseurs. Perhaps it was a muscle spasm, caused by my major surgery last year, that made me miss my footing on the stairs going up to street level. Needless to say I received no sympathy from my travel companion. Personally I think he stepped way over the mark when he explained to the rest of the passengers, " It's OK he's been drinking all day ".
John; So we wandered down to the 'Horse Shoe' bar and had only one pint there, I think. Then it was back on the train, slept all the way to EK, woke up refreshed, and walked up to the 'Monty'. We had a couple of pints there and then Kate picked us up (I phoned her) and took us home.
So ended another great trip during which we saw the past in the shape of the Renfrew ferry and future in the shape of a Bus that can, or can't, go on water, only time will tell.

Our spends for the day;

Bus fares	Zero
Renfrew Ferry	Zero
Boat Fares	£2.40
Train Fares	£4.00 approx (can't remember)
Food (fish supper)	£5.10 (some price)
Drink	£30.00 (can't admit to any more)
Total	**£41.50**

Post Script; *A couple of weeks after our historic journey it was announced that a new Renfrew Ferry would be taking over the ancient route. There would be no break in service as only the operator would change. That was great news. However in a very annoying twist we discovered that since it was now effectively privatised we no longer qualified for free travel on it. If this new ferry ever gets into trouble they can just forget about calling on us for support.*

Capital Punishment

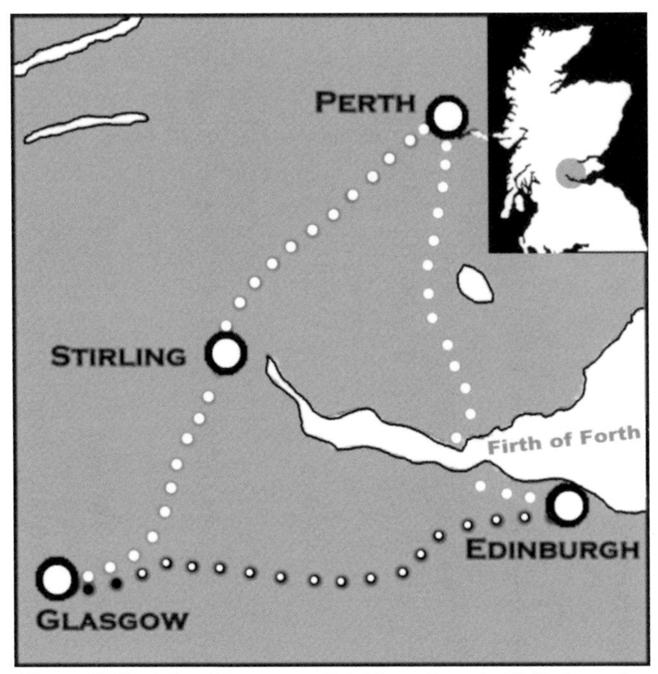

East Kilbride-Glasgow-Stirling-Perth-Edinburgh-Glasgow-East Kilbride
(Four Buses, Two Trains)

John; I called this our City Trip, but Craig overruled with Capital Punishment as going to Edinburgh is always a punishment for him. One of our reasons for this trip was that the weather had been terrible for the last four months, so if it was a bad day, we would always be in big towns, meaning near pubs. After almost four months of miserable weather, it was a scorcher, the best day for months.
So we set off with light hearts and heavy wallets, as a good few pubs would be visited.

We got the number 18 bus from just outside Craig's house right into Buchanan Street Bus Station. This is a new route for the 18 and very handy for us oldies. After wandering about the bus station wondering if we should get a different bus from the one planned, we decided, as the other bus had not turned up, to get the planned M8 which was going to Dundee via Stirling and Perth. It was a nice journey with the only talking point being the architectural nightmare which is Cumbernauld Town Centre. It makes East Kilbrides' centre look nice, and that's saying something.

So we journeyed up to Stirling, passing Bannockburn, where Mel Gibson beat the English. It all looked very nice in the sunshine.

We got off at Stirling Bus Station about ten to eleven, which gave us ten minutes to be tourists before the pubs opened.

Craig; *The Stirling, Perth and Edinburgh trip was one of our better planned journeys. We were confident that we had covered all the possibilities. With only three main destinations, all contained in a tight circular route not a lot could go wrong, could it?*

Of the three towns Stirling was the one I was looking forward to most. I've been there many times and have some very good memories of the place.

Perth on the other hand was always just a name on a road sign to me. I have, until now always managed to by-pass the town on my way to somewhere else more interesting.

Edinburgh is a city I could well do without visiting ever again. This is not because Edinburgh's citizens are unfriendly, unhelpful or pretentious. Although you could make a good argument for that case. No, my aversion to Edinburgh is mostly medical. Last year I had my operation in the city's Royal Infirmary and every time the city's name

is mentioned in conversation I get phantom pains in my side.
I was less than impressed with our driver on the Glasgow to Stirling leg of our journey. When the time came to leave our bus stance his limitations became apparent. He managed to stall the bus three times before someone came over to show him how to engage the reverse gear. I don't think I'm being picky but surely the proper use of gears must feature quite strongly in the driving test for passenger vehicles.
Maybe it was because ours was not a peak time bus, and therefore full of non-paying oldies, that we got a second string driver. Possibly, between the hours of 9am and 3pm the buses are staffed by drivers who were borderline test failures. Since we are travelling for free we can't really complain. We can only hope that even if our partially trained driver doesn't know much about gears he has at least read the chapter in his manual headed "the efficient use of brakes". The journey to Stirling was very scenic and thankfully accident free.
I'm not sure if it was the heat or just the excitement but John was a little confused as we entered Stirling. We were just passing the historic site of the battle of Bannockburn when John announced, to anyone within earshot, that Mel Gibson had defeated the English on this very spot. I'm pretty sure he meant the late great Ayrshire man Sir William Wallace. The fact that it was King Robert the Bruce who actually did the business with the Sassenachs is neither here nor there. We had more important matters to deal with.
The magical hour was upon us. It was eleven o'clock, opening time. After a quick attempt at soaking up some local culture by way of a couple of old turreted buildings and a statue of the afore mentioned W. Wallace we made our way to our first pub of the day.

Sir William Wallace, patriot, freedom fighter and well known Ayrshireman

John; As I know the centre of Stirling fairly well (my youngest Gregor went to university here) I led the way up to the scenic touristy bit with the cobbled stones and narrow streets.

We spotted about four pubs right away and decided to go first into one called 'Nicky Tams'. It was nice in a very touristy/studenty way, but the barman, owner I think, was an ex EK man, so that was ok. After a very nice pint, we ventured across the road and into the 'Claymore'. This was completely different. It was an old man's pub with a few young men who, to quote one of the locals 'were all on

invalidity'. Good job they didn't hear him say this or they would have chased him out of the pub and attacked him with their walking sticks. They certainly looked fit enough, the lazy bastards. If the government stopped paying them not to work, the pubs would be empty.
The wee man who told us this also spoke to us for a while and informed us that he had a girlfriend in Bearsden and was still up for it. Just what you want to hear early in the day.

John enjoys a brew in Nicky Tams

The pint here was not as good as in the previous pub, so we obviously had to get a decider, so we ventured into the 'No. 2 Baker Street'. This pub was situated somewhere near the start of Baker Street and was more like one of these modern pubs that encourage children and other unwelcome sorts. The pint was reasonable and the artificial fire was roaring. Didn't like the place at all.

So after a wee walk down through a bit of scenic grandeur, passing a statue of William Wallace (he is the real Mel Gibson), we found ourselves back at the bus station and got on the 12.43pm M8 bus to Perth. I had my pieces on the bus, cheese and pickle, and then I think I slept the rest of the way, because we seemed to get there in no time at all.

Craig; *Nicky Tams' appeared to be a theme pub. Our problem was that we couldn't quite work out what the theme was. The best I could come up with was it seemed to be an interactive depiction of the local boozer in Brigadoon.*

Being the first customers of the day meant we suffered the fate of all enthusiastic beer swiggers. We got all the rubbish that was left in the pipes from the night before. Well that's my explanation of the pint of pish I was served.

Next to receive a visit from us was the Claymore. It was the complete opposite of our last refreshment stop. The Claymore was what I think is nowadays described as minimalist. The less charitable would probably call it cheap and nasty. Certainly there was very little in the way of décor but, the minimalist theme was carried on by the pub's clientele. They didn't seem to have much going for them.

I might be wrong here but I don't think the Claymore has a quiz team. Certainly not one that requires shelf space in the pub for its winners' trophies. Their blank stares when we entered were matched by their blank surroundings.

We had only been in the place a minute or so before we made a new friend. His name escapes me. He couldn't wait to give us a short history of his life so far. I think John attracts these kind of people. Although this bloke spoke with a pronounced English accent he claimed that he was originally from Aberdeen. One of us, I don't know who, asked him why he came to Stirling instead of going back to Aberdeen when he moved back to Scotland. In answer he

told us never to go to Aberdeen as the entire city was inhabited by arseholes. I had always suspected this to be true, but here was proof positive.
One pint was enough for us and we moved on.
Our next port of call was No2 Baker Street I was not impressed. The pub is, I imagine, one of those 'corporate' or branded bars. It was decorated in a mixture of modern and traditional styles. The traditional elements were of course fake while the modern ones were just boring. I couldn't make up my mind whether it was supposed to be a wine bar, a sports bar or a Scottish theme pub drawn from the imagination of a recent art school graduate.
Thankfully it was time to head up to Perth.
John; Perth was a big let down. All you hear about it is that it is a great place to live and very nice etc, but the area round about the bus station is pretty shitty looking, even on a lovely day. However, this didn't matter as we are only looking for a good pub. We wandered into 'Delights'. It wasn't really a delight, but the beer was not bad and we passed a pleasant one pint. The locals did not seem very talkative, or maybe no ones up to it in Perth. We left and wandered around a bit and found an Irish pub called 'The Auld Hoose'. It was no more Irish than me. It was not a bad pub though and we enjoyed the pint and the craic (that's what you're supposed to say).
The trip then started to fall apart. We got to the bus station a couple of minutes before the bus was due only to find it had gone. What a bummer! All we could do was find another pub locally. 'The Rabbie Burns' fitted the bill and although a bit rough, we fitted in perfectly and enjoyed a pint while ranting on about buses which can't keep to a timetable.
Craig; *I suppose it's only fair that bus stations are always built in less well developed areas. The good sites obviously*

attract higher ground rents. But building them in side streets means it takes forever to get to them. It seemed to me that maybe the driver didn't quite know where the bus station actually was. I'm fairly sure we passed the same line of grotty looking shops a couple of times before we arrived at our stop. Then again maybe Perth just has more than its fair share of grotty looking shops.

All this circling around narrow back streets had a devastating effect on John's pub navigation system. That at least, was his excuse for charging off in the opposite direction to all things alcoholic.

Our accidental field trip brought us to the entrance to the railway station. This gave John the inspired idea that we could take the train to Edinburgh instead of the bus. A change to the railway meant we would be crossing over the world famous Forth Rail Bridge. Fantastic.

A quick check on the cost of a ticket soon changed our minds. I don't remember the exact price but I'm pretty sure we could have hired a helicopter for a fairly similar amount.

Eventually we found what we were really looking for; a pub. Our first pub was called Dickens Bar. It is in quite an imposing four storey building. From the outside it looks very classy. Inside it's not so classy. Maybe they ran out of money tarting up the outside. We did enjoy our pints in Dickens and I suppose that's all that really matters.

After a quick shuffle round the narrow streets we found an Irish pub. It was called the Auld Hoose. At least that's what it said on the front. Just for a dash of authenticity the sign on the side of the building read 'an seann taigh'. Presumably that's in case you didn't clock the fact it was supposed to be an Irish pub. It was the only Irish thing about the place.

We had an itinerary to keep to so we dragged ourselves away from the Auld Hoose and made our way back to the

Dickens Bar, quite literally no that good.

bus station. What a pity the bus company doesn't seem as keen to stick to their timetables. It's bad enough missing your bus because you were a bit slow letting go of your bar stool but, when it's the bus company who buggers things up, it's maddening.

The Edinburgh bus was nowhere to be seen. Another would be passenger asked me if I'd seen the bus. He told me he had been waiting twenty minutes for the same bus and hadn't seen any sign of it.

We had some time to kill, and we knew how to kill it.

The Robert Burns Lounge was our pub of choice. In contrast to the fake Irish bar this little place was one hundred percent genuinely Scottish. That is to say, it was a bit of a dump. I liked it. The décor was very definitely on the shabby side. Possibly the last time it was freshened up would have been for the opening ceremony. Maybe Rabbie himself did the

honours. It did however have two saving graces. The beer was good and it was reasonably priced.
Given that this wee pub was only fifty yards away from our first stop, Dickens Bar, I think we will have to admit that we didn't exactly do an in depth study of the Perth pub scene.
At our second attempt we managed to get onto the bus to Edinburgh. What really surprised me was the bus was not very busy. I would like to know what happened to all the passengers who missed the previous one.
John; The bus we got was the M9, which was different to the M8 which we were planning to get. It wandered through every wee village on the way and took forever. The only saving grace was that we got a fantastic view of The Forth Bridge.

The First Forth Bridge

It was a laugh trying to take photos from a moving bus. Craig is a bit of a perfectionist with his big camera which, although it takes great pictures, needs about an hour to set up each shot. No use when racing over a bridge. Funny how he managed to get a good photo then. Think I talk a load of crap.

We arrived into Edinburgh and managed to get off the bus before the terminus, just at the start (or one end) of Rose Street. This is a street famous for having about a thousand pubs along its length. The first one we visited was 'The Kenilworth' which was very nice. The beer was good and we had a nice wee chat with a local who was interested in our day out. He must lead a right boring life. Leaving this pub we headed along Rose Street, passing a few pubs before settling for one called 'The Auld Hundred'. This was more of a lounge bar type place, but we got a seat at the bar and had our pint. I must mention that the price of drink is going up at a hell of a rate. We were paying a fortune for a pint. You pay well over a fiver for two pints. A couple of years ago I could get drunk for a fiver. This government are a shower of robbers who have no idea of how to get money other that to up taxes on bevy. Here's an idea, cut out social security and money for druggies and we could afford a pint again. Of course if they suggested that, they would lose the vote of the majority of the country, who are all now non-working, lazy bastards.

We then stopped ranting and made our way down to Waverley Station for the train home. Can't risk the bus after a few pints. Although there was a rail strike of sorts on, the rail company assured us that the Edinburgh to Glasgow service would not be affected. Pretty crap strike if you ask me. In the old days we knew how to organise a strike, or actually Craig did, I was usually in management.

So as we arrived at the station it all went dark, a power cut. There's more than one way to stop the trains. So we asked the man at the gate, who said he had no idea what was happening or when any trains would run, certainly none in the short term. Not the type to panic, we wandered back up to Rose Street and went in the first pub we came to and had

a couple of pints while discussing what we should do. I sent a text to Kate, telling her of our terrible situation, "this means more drink". That was the gist of Kate's reply.
So in a state of apprehension (drunk) we wandered back to the station and found out that the panic was over, so I bought two singles at a vending machine. Tickets were over a tenner each. What's that all about. So much for the cheap way round! No discount or anything, it's a bloody disgrace. I am going to write to somebody.
Craig; *Edinburgh is not my favourite place but, it does have it's compensations. Rose Street is legendary among serious drinkers. It has a very impressive pub to shop ratio.*
Perhaps it was just because it was getting near to the end of a long day's travelling or, maybe it was my aversion to all things Edinburgh. but, I didn't enjoy either of the two pubs we visited.
Down at Waverley Station we got a bit of a shock. All the destination boards were blank, all the lights were out and all the trains were going nowhere.
For the second time that day we were forced to take refuge in a pub because of a transport glitch. The rail strike was a bit of a nuisance but it was also a pathetic example of industrial action. There were no picket lines, no burning braziers and not even a hint of threatening behaviour. I, for one, was glad there was no picket line as I would find it hard to cross, even to get home. John, on the other hand would probably have enjoyed crossing it. Being a former management oppressor, it's in the blood.
Back at the station all the lights were back on. Ditto the trains. The train back to Glasgow was packed but we still managed to get a few minutes sleep. That refreshed us enough to make a detour to the Horse Shoe for a couple of night caps.

A refreshing stroll along Rose Street

The trip had not exactly gone to plan but, there was little we could have done to alter that. All the boxes were ticked and we made it back to East Kilbride more or less on time.

John; So we slept all the way back to Glasgow, and as it was very late by now, although I have no idea how late, we decided we would get straight to the Central Station and onto the first train. Our walk took us right past 'The Horse Shoe', so we got the later train home. Not really our fault, is it?

Craig had contacted Irene, telling her what train we would get. Don't think he mentioned The Horse Shoe though, and she picked us up and took me right to my door. What a woman, and lucky too!

So ended another enjoyable trip round Scotland.

Trips financial details;

Bus Fares;	Zero
Train Fares;	£10.40 (Waverley no more)
Food;	£1.40 chips from Blue Dolphin
Drink;	£25.00 about 10 pints, not proud
Total;	**£36.80 (getting out of hand)**

Memories of old Killie

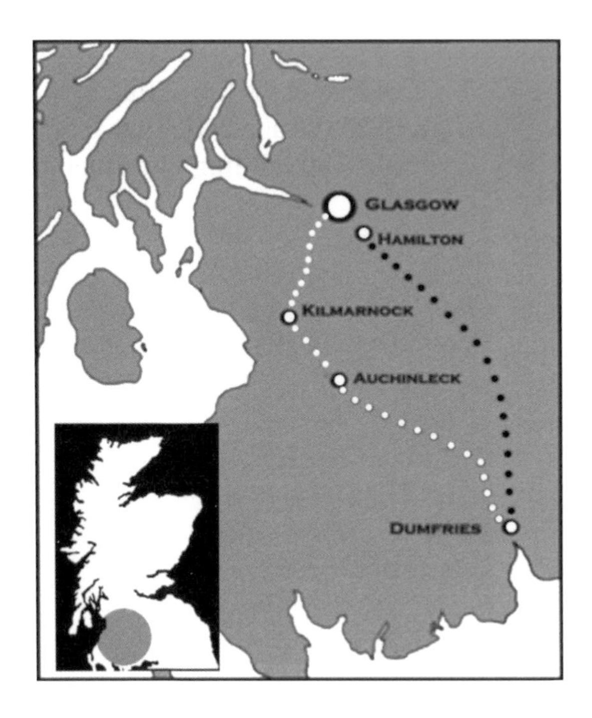

East Kilbride-Hamilton-Dumfries-Auchinleck-Glasgow-East Kilbride
(Two Buses, Three Trains)

John; We had been talking about a visit South for quite a while, taking in Craig's birthplace Auchinleck. So on a glorious Monday morning (14th June) we set off to the land of Burns, Miners, Farmers and supporters of *'The Talbot'*, Auchinleck's Junior football team. Junior football is very big in Ayrshire and separates towns and even families and friends.

Irene, Craig's long suffering partner, ran us to the bus station, although it's only a ten minute walk. What a woman! Kate (the wife) was snoring in bed. Our original plan was to visit Cumnock and New Cumnock as well as the towns mentioned above, but Craig had Googled them and stated they looked shut. The truth is he hates all Ayrshire towns that are not Auchinleck.

Our first bus was the 205 to Hamilton, although I think we might have taken another one which arrived first. I'm not sure-who cares.

After me buying Craig strong mints at Hamilton bus station, we got on the 9.25am X74 to Dumfries. It was a lovely journey, even the M74 looks good from your higher viewpoint on the bus.

For some reason the bus stopped about three or four times and the driver shot out of the bus, only to arrive back a few seconds later looking worried. We reckon he had a weak bladder or there was something wrong with the bus.

Another thing that was worrying me was that because we were missing out two Ayrshire towns, the bus from Dumfries to Auchinleck would take about an hour and a half, with no toilet. So after much discussion we decided to get the train from Dumfries to Glasgow, getting off at Auchinleck and Kilmarnock. This meant we had longer in Dumfries, about two pints longer than if we had got the bus, so all was well. Due to a bout of tiredness (pissed) I didn't find out till the next day, when checking the photographs, that we had actually been in a pub in Kilmarnock. It's a worry!

Craig; *Our latest journey must rank as the least well planned expedition ever. It wasn't just a case of a few last minute arrangements, we managed to improvise at every single stage of the trip. The only piece of planning which*

Three men very set in their ways

remained unbuggered about with was our lift back up the road from the 'Monty' at journey's end.

I would like to say that most of the chopping and changing was down to John, but that would just be a classic bit of blame shifting. No, it was all my doing. In my own defence, I did have good reason to be a bit nervous about this trip. We were going to Auchinleck after all.

For years now I've been bragging about my old home town, being certain that no one up in East Kilbride knew much about the place. My bluff was about to be called.

My potential downfall came about in the usual way. Alcohol plays far too big a part in our planning processes. The strategy meetings we hold occasionally always take place in

a pub, usually at the end of the evening. The dangers are obvious. In this instance I think someone must have switched my tipple of choice, Tennant's lager, for several litres of 'Stella'. It's the only explanation I can come up with.
We managed to get Irene to give us a lift down to the bus station. This, like almost everything else that day, was not part of the original plan because we were now at the station earlier than we expected to be.
John suggested that, rather than hang around waiting, we take a different bus to Hamilton. It didn't make much difference but, maybe that was when the rot set in.
The coach taking us down to Dumfries was quite comfortable. Especially after we found seats which were not being blasted by freezing air from the broken ceiling vents.
For some unexplained reason the driver kept stopping the bus and getting out. What he was doing out there was a mystery. The more he did it the more bizarre our suggestions got. Bladder problems were our first guess. Eventually I convinced myself that there was something wrong with the bus. I'm not exactly sure what an axle bearing is, or even if there is such a thing, but I was certain I could smell one burning.
After about an hour we drove into the town of Moffat. It looked really nice. The bus stopped in what I take it was the town square and I was relieved to note that none of the locals were pointing at the bus wheels and screaming.
I suggested to John that Moffat might make a good destination for one of our trips. On the way in I had counted at least four pubs, so it definitely qualified.
The remainder of the journey to Dumfies was incident free. Only when we got into the town itself did anything go wrong. I think it could have been road works or something but we lost some precious time, time we couldn't afford. We had

planned to spend only an hour in Dumfries but now we didn't even have that much time.
Deciding there was no time to lose we ditched our plans to soak up some of the culture of this historic market town and proceed to soak up some beer instead.
Ye Old Friars Vaults was a strange looking little pub from the outside. Fortunately for us it was a strange little pub on the inside as well. Stepping through the doors of the Vaults was a bit like stepping back in time.
A one word description of the décor would be beige, everything was beige. We found out from the customers that because the pub is so close to the River Nith it gets flooded on a regular basis. River residue might explain the colour scheme. It might also explain why there was so little furniture in the place. I did notice that the tables were bolted to the floor.
The landlady told us that she could no longer get flood water insurance. Before I could stop myself I suggested that the next time they got a flood warning she should get some of her customers to set fire to the place. She was not amused.
Looking round the place I would imagine 50 quid and a couple of thousand Nectar points would have the old place looking as good as new.
Despite the risk of sudden flooding we bravely decided to have another pint. It was at this point, and by mutual agreement, we opted to let the train take the strain. We also learned a valuable life lesson here. Never ask for directions in a pub. Especially when said pub is inhabited by the 3 Stooges. The trio at the bar managed to give us 3 totally different 'shortest' routes to the railway station. Actually it was only two. The tallest of the men didn't count as a source of information as we couldn't make out a word he said. I don't know if he was suffering from too much booze, too

much sun or a bad misjudgement in his medication. He made the other two men appear almost normal.
Once again I found it doesn't take much to get total strangers to reveal their inner most thoughts. A couple of beers usually does the trick. My new best friend was soon telling me all about how he would rescue the economy, end terrorism and return Britain to super power status. Actually he was beginning to sound a bit like John, only more rabid. A loose explanation of his theory would be to get rid of everyone unfortunate enough to have skin any darker than his own.
I got the impression that he thought Enoch Powell might have had some of the right ideas but had been too much of a left wing bleeding heart to carry them out. It was time to leave.
John; We got off the at the bus station in Dumfries and went round the corner and came across a wee pub on the corner called '*ye Old Friars Vaults'* , so in we went and as it was the back of eleven and the pub was just open, we got the usual smell of bleach to make you think they have cleaned the place. And what a place it was. The pub itself was nice, the price list was made from what looked like multi coloured lego bricks, but as the drink was to quote, 'the cheapest in Dumfries' we ordered a couple of pints. The amazing thing about the pub was the other four regulars were all completely mad or demented.
One of the guys must have been a helicopter pilot in a previous life. He shouted all the time, but you had no idea what he was saying. We just had to smile and say things like 'you're right there and no problem big man'. Another one was like a bigot from 20 years ago. It was unbelievable some of the things he was saying. I am not what you would call politically correct, but I was shocked. The other two guys

The Old Friars Vaults, aka The Asylum Bar

were not so crazy, but were still great fun.

The woman who was the landlady was very good and kept the locals in order and did not let them get too excited. The national health would save a fortune on Vallium if the nurses were as good as the landlady.

This is a pub worth a visit if you are ever stuck in Dumfries.

We asked for directions to the Train Station, and had ordered and finished a pint before everyone in the pub had a go at telling how to get there. What a laugh! But it was a great wee pub and would recommend it to anyone, especially if you like getting shouted at.

So with heavy hearts, we left '*the Vaults*' and wandered up the road following the instructions given to us. About halfway there, we passed a pub called '*The Hole In The Wa'*, Craig said this was a famous pub and we had to go in. He seemed to convince me no problem. The entrance was dead atmospheric, through a close, but when we got in it was just like a new wave pub with wide screen tellies and all that crap you get in modern pubs. We had a pint anyway, which was about twice the price of '*the Vaults*' and wandered up to the Train Station. By the way, Dumfries is just like any other wee town, half the shops were shut and the place was full of jakies, although not as many as wander about East Kilbride talking through their noses.

The wee woman in the station ticket office was very helpful, although she never smiled (one out of two in Scotland is not bad) and sold us tickets to Glasgow, although we were allowed to get off and on as often as we liked. We still had about half an hour to kill, so we walked across the road and into a bar called '*The Waverley*', which advertised a beer garden. Beer garden my arse. These places just put two seats outside for smokers. There was a big Station Hotel opposite the station, funnily enough, which would have had a nice beer garden, but Craig reckoned the word Waverley meant something to me as '*The Waverley*' was a Clyde River Steamer. I am still a member of the CRSC. I pay the fees every year, although I must go to a meeting soon.

So we finished our pint, wandered over to the station and ate our pieces on the platform in the sunshine, I had Corned Beef, as normal.

The train arrived, it was a wee two carriage one, just like the East Kilbride one. Funny how I thought it would be a big train since it was going a long way. It had a toilet, which I used (four pints had been downed by then).

Craig; *On our walk up to the station I spied the historic Hole in the Wa' pub. I'm a real sucker for history don't you know. For more years than I care to remember I have wanted to visit this pub. Maybe because I had been looking forward to it for so long I had built up this picture in my mind of what it would be like. The image shattered as soon as we entered. There were no olde worlde knick knacks on the walls, no*

The Hole in the Wa. Pity it wasn't a hole in the ground

roaring log fire and no seven piece folk group playing earthy tunes in the corner. It was just an ordinary pub. It was rubbish. One pint later we were on the move again.

Despite all the directions we were given by the vault dwellers we found the railway station with little bother.

Hard faced is not a description I would generally use to describe anyone, but sometimes it's unavoidable. The lady at the ticket desk in the station defied any other description. To the best of my knowledge neither John or me had ever set eyes on the woman, let alone grossly insulted her. The expression on her face suggested otherwise. We got our tickets, apologised for annoying her by being there and left.

To get over the trauma of having our faces bitten off we decided to have another beer.

The Waverley Bar was just across the road and it had a beer garden. It seemed like a good idea, sitting outside in the shade, drinking ice cold beer. This beer garden didn't live up to my expectations. It would take a fairly warped mind to describe this giant ashtray as a beer garden. The busy road junction alongside did nothing to help the atmosphere. A panoramic view of the used car lot across the street rounded off the experience. As a small postscript to all of that, the beer wasn't very cold.

John; It was a lovely journey through Burns country, whatever that means. The atmosphere was building up as we approached the famed Auchinleck and I was not disappointed. What a dump! Even in the sunshine it was depressing, although I told Craig it was a great wee place. It was his round and I didn't want to upset him, not in his beloved Auchinleck. The first pub we visited was 'The Boswell Arms'. If there had been a piano player, he would have stopped. There were four men sitting at the bar looking really depressed. After about ten minutes of them ignoring us, it turned out that two of the guys new Craig. They didn't like him, but knew him. One of them was related to Craig through marriage, I think. Auchinleck's not a place that strangers ask the locals anything that might be in any way personal. This was the first time Craig had been back in the place for about 15 years.

In the second pub, which was called '*the Railway Hotel'* nobody seemed to know Craig, but Craig reckoned one of them was his brother, or maybe not. Like the first pub, this was not a nice place.

Everything brightened up when we went across the road and into 'The Market Inn'. Everyone (or a couple of people) knew Craig. It was handshakes all round and it's your turn to buy a round Craig.

One of Craig's closest friends from the past heard he was in town and came in. What a great time we had, so much so that we missed the train we had planned to get. So we decided to get the later train and give Kilmarnock a miss, or so I thought. It's not Auchinleck after all. So it was back to the pub for more back slapping and having a great time, even I was enjoying myself, I usually do after about 10 pints.

Eventually we had to leave to much sorrow and the singing of Burns songs. I was beginning to like Auchinleck.

We stopped at some fast food place on the way to the station and got God only knows what. It was crap. The seagulls got most of it.

Craig; *The journey up from Dumfries was very pleasant. I enjoyed the scenery and John enjoyed the toilet facilities. We had decided to give New Cumnock a miss and go straight on to Auchinleck.*

I was glad the sun was shining as the old town could do with all the help it could get. Mining towns weren't built to look pretty. The train guard seemed to think it was hilarious that Auchinleck was now attracting a couple of tourists.

We took the scenic route from the station which passes the site of the old Highhouse pit and the site of the miners' rows where I was born. At the top of this road sits the Barony Church. It was here that I managed to gain a rather odd claim to fame. Not many people have been asked to leave a wedding service half way through the ceremony. I was. The minister took exception to me filming the service and stopped the wedding until I left the building. Very embarrassing.

Our first pub was the Boswell Arms. Needless to say I've had many a good session in this place in the past. Unfortunately today wasn't going to add to the total.

The bar had been changed around a bit since the last time I'd been there. I couldn't say the same for the customers. Not for the first time that day I was struck by how old these people had become. I, myself, haven't aged a day.
It was hardly a hero's welcome I received. A couple of the drinkers did acknowledge my existence, but only grudgingly. One of them was a cousin of a cousin of mine and I just about recognised him. John must have felt pretty strange. Actually if he had been he would have been right at home in this pub. Not a lot of laughs it has to be said. One pint was enough. In fact, without a word being spoken, we were both drinking quite a bit faster than normal.
As we made our way up the street we noticed that there was not much business going on. It seemed to me the only growth industries in the town were hairdressers and tanning salons. The same could be said for most small towns nowadays.
Up at the other end of town we visited The Railway Hotel. Newcomers to the town are often confused when locals talk about this place. It has had so many names in the recent past that sometimes all of them could be used in a single conversation. Danny's, the Auchinleck Arms and Dick's, often called Dirty Dick's., have all been used at some time. After explaining all this to John it was a great disappointment to find the bar was like death's waiting room. In fact I'm pretty sure one or two of the customers were in the early stages of decomposition. I knew a few of the old codgers in there but I'm pretty sure I got away unrecognised. Of course there were one or two of the customers in there who wouldn't recognise themselves in a mirror. The last pub in town is called the Market Inn, although, this being Auchinleck, it is better known as 'the Mad Hoose.'

Craig about to be struck by lightning

This may or may not give you an idea of the type of clientele to be found within.
When we entered the pub I recognised quite a few of the customers. Once again I was shocked to see how old these guys had become in the years since I last saw them. The welcome here was a lot warmer than the other two pubs and it was good to talk to some old friends. I'm not sure what John was making of all this and I was a wee bit concerned that he wasn't enjoying his day out. Although a constant supply of Tennant's 70/- seemed to keep him amused.
Perhaps if we'd come in a couple of hours earlier some of the customers would have been easier to understand. As it was some of them were on to advanced Latin, or at least that's what it sounded like.

I managed to get in contact with a very good friend of mine from the town and he managed to meet up with us in the bar. It was a great little reunion. Somehow, and I can't imagine why, we managed to miss our train. We were forced through no fault of our own to spend another two hours in the pub.
Before going for our train we decided to get ourselves some food as it had been a while since we'd had our sandwiches. That's why we ended up in the Tandoori Take Away. We'd had a fair amount of beer by this time so we thought it would be safer to stick to a couple of portions of chips. I'm fairly certain that there would be more nutritional value in eating the polystyrene box than the chips. It would be a toss up as to which was tastier.
Next stop Kilmarnock. This is where things get a little complicated. John has no recollection of us stopping off in Kilmarnock, while my memory is fairly clear. When we got off the train we crossed the road to the wonderfully named 'Fanny by Gaslight'. How could anyone forget going into a place with that name? Perhaps John was suffering from sleep deprivation. The pub itself, if not by name, was pretty ordinary. Maybe we were not seeing it at its best. It could be that it really has to be seen by gaslight. Very low gaslight.
John; So it was back on the train to Glasgow for a sleep. We arrived in Glasgow about 8.30pm and Craig talked me into going to *'The Horse Shoe'* for a pint. At least that's how I remembered it. We would have had a thirst on us by then. I have little recollection of the rest of the night. I know we got the train to EK, we walked to *'The Monty'* for one more drink, and Craig managed to talk Irene into coming and picking us up. The next thing I knew it was tomorrow.
What a trip.

Craig; *John had a really good sleep on the train and woke refreshed and ready for a bit of a night cap in the Horse Shoe before the short journey home.*

Cost for the day; (all very approx)

Bus fares	Zero
Train fares	£12.50
Food (gross)	£3.00 (I think)
Drink	£30.00 (must have had about 12 pints)
Total	**£45.50 (got to cut out the food)**

Worlds Smallest Harbour my Arse

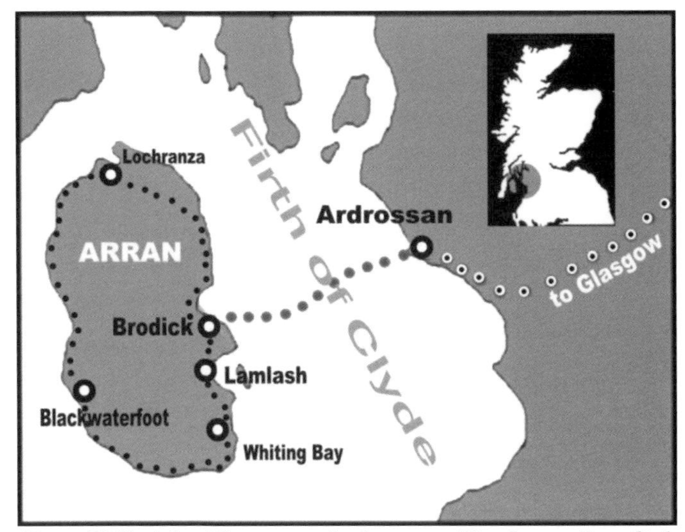

East Kilbride-Glasgow-Ardrossan Harbour-Brodick
Blackwaterfoot-Whiting Bay-Lamlash-Brodick
Ardrossan Harbour-Glasgow-East Kilbride
(Four Trains, Two Ferries, Four Buses)

John; The idea of this trip (Craig's' idea) was to go right round Arran on the bus, stopping at various places to view the scenic grandeur, but in reality to have a few pints. The cheap way round bit took a hammering as it cost about £20 each to get to Arran. Buses could not be used because of time constraints and Arran being an Island!
At about 7.15am, Kate (the wife) drove us down to East Kilbride station for the 7.25am train. As my pensioners' card doesn't work till after nine, but Craig's (I'm ill card!) does, he very generously insisted that we half the total so we were paying the same. That's what friends are for.

Craig; *Our latest adventure promised to be our most expensive yet. The Isle of Arran, in the Clyde Estuary, is only 55 miles in circumference but it would take us most of the day to travel round. The buses of course would be free, courtesy of the government, but we would also need to use four trains and two ferries.*

Although it was my idea to go to Arran I didn't really think it through properly. Once we checked the train and sailing times I realised that it was going to be a very early start. This was bad news for me as it has been pointed out, more than a few times, that I'm not at my best first thing in the morning. Actually I need a good half hour to myself, just to sit and stare into space.

To get to John's place for our 7.15 departure I calculated that I would need to set the alarm for 6 o'clock. That's the middle of the night as far as I'm concerned. As it turned out I needn't have bothered. I didn't sleep a wink all night.

When we arrived at the station in East Kilbride the train was already in, so we hurried to the ticket office. I got my ticket and went onto the platform. John decided to interrogate the poor wee bloke behind the desk. He was trying to get the best deal possible.

Meanwhile I was pacing up and down outside the train hoping I wouldn't have to block the doors to stop it from leaving without us. I usually buy a newspaper to read on the train, John makes do with the Daily Mail, but as time was limited I couldn't risk going to the kiosk. Safely on the train we settled back to enjoy the first leg of our latest trip. Needless to say the train sat there for another five minutes.

John; After wandering around Glasgow Central for about half an hour and buying a couple of cans of juice for a pound, we boarded the 8.33am to Ardrossan Harbour.

The only thing of note on the train journey was at Saltcoats when a young guy came on with lovely twin boys about four years old. They sat down and he started to talk. It was obvious he was a drug addict and jakey, talking nonsense and through his nose. One nostril already gone. What chance do these boys have-none.

Craig; *Down in Glasgow we had time to buy a paper. For a change John bought a copy of the Daily Record, just for me he said. On the Ardrossan train we debated the merits of our favoured newspapers. John described my choice, the Record and the Herald, as left wing rags. While I suggested his cherished Daily Mail wasn't fit to wrap chips in. We called it a draw and moved on to more important topics, namely the antics of our fellow travellers.*

The only ones worth mentioning were the 'jakies' who got on at Saltcoats. They were run of the mill knuckle draggers, all tattoos and gold chains. Personally I regret the demise of the shell suit. Back in it's heyday all the numpties wore them. It was like a uniform for them.

However it was their kids who were most annoying. From the moment they got on they set about hurling themselves around the carriage. They jumped on the seats, rolled around the floor and screamed like banshees. They must be mainlining 'Sunny Delight' on a regular basis. Luckily for us the whole tribe of them got off at the next stop.

John; We arrived at Ardrossan Harbour and having done this sail before, knew the routine of buying tickets and finding the bar on the ferry. I'm not proud of it, but we were first to the bar when the ferry sailed.

The Ferry was called 'Eileanan Chaledonia' for the benefit of Scotland's two Gaelic speakers or 'Caledonian Isles' for the rest of us. By the way, I read just recently that the Scottish Government were under pressure to stop wasting hundreds of thousands of taxpayers money putting every sign in the country in Gaelic as well as English. Now there's an idea I could have given them years ago. Why shouldn't the Gaelic speakers have their taxes used for the English signs?

A lovely sail and a couple of pints later we arrived in Brodick, I must say Brodick is not the most attractive of places, it is very bitty, no two buildings are the same and looks as if it has been thrown together.

With our previous ferry experience we managed to get off quickly by sneaking round the side of the queue and only annoying a couple of people, and as people are usually afraid of grumpy old men, it was no problem.

All aboard for the booze cruise

Craig; *Once aboard the Arran ferry we made straight for the bar, predictably some might say. I like to think we were doing a public service. Although a lot of people would like to have a small refreshment when they get on board there is an embarrassment factor to overcome. The stigma of being first* *in the queue at the bar can be too much for some delicate souls. John was actually standing at the bar when the grill was raised.*

I was enjoying my second pint, with not a care in the world, when I noticed the boat had stopped moving. Turning round I saw that we had reached Brodick and were in fact tying up at the pier. I'd been looking out the wrong window. We made a quick exit.

John; We managed to get seats on the No. 324 which ended up packed with people standing. Funnily enough I still feel guilty at not offering someone my seat. You cannot beat the old 'Boys Brigade' upbringing. All the tourists got off at the cheese and whisky making places and the walkers got off at Goat Fell (Arran's' highest hill).

Craig mentioned on the journey that he thought the driver was from Poland, or somewhere like that, (Craig has a history of stand up fights with Poles). This was proved to be true when an English tourist asked him a question when getting off the bus. He replied 'I'm from another place', or something like that. The lady just grabbed a timetable and stormed off the bus. Arran must do more than just employ people who can drive as it's entire existence relies on tourists, most of them English, as are most of the population.

During this entire trip, by the way, I had to listen to Craig telling me that he had walked, cycled, but mainly pushed his bike all round the island. I answered with the usual, 'that's great', or 'what a feat'. It kept him happy.

Craig; *It is a 45 minute bus journey from Brodick to Lochranza. Having walked this road I can thoroughly recommend taking the bus.*

While planning this trip it was decided that we would miss out Lochranza as a refreshment stop. There were 2 reasons for this. The first was that we could not find a bus that would let us continue on down the West coast after visiting the town. Reason number two, and the most important one in my opinion, was that Lochranza was not worth the effort. That might seem a little unfair but in my defence I have been there a couple of times before.

There is a ruined castle and a hotel near the centre of the town. I was once grossly over charged in the hotel, so it is forever off limits to me. As far as the castle goes, when you've seen one old ruin you've seen one too many.

Speaking of old ruins, John really enjoyed the journey down the coast as he had never seen this side of the island. I myself have travelled this road many times, on the bus, bike and of course by foot. To entertain John I recounted the stories of my many journeys, in great detail. The bus driver added to the excitement of the occasion by driving like a loony. How he managed to get the bus past that petrol tanker on a road which couldn't have been more than ten feet wide amazed us both.

We intended getting off the bus at the Kinloch Hotel. My reason for choosing it was that it sits next to the bus stop. Unfortunately no one had informed the driver about the curious notion of buses stopping at bus stops. We panicked.

I think he felt sorry for us and stopped just along the road near the second of our target destinations. The Blackwaterfoot Lodge is a great wee pub. Most of the time.

John; So by the time we arrived at our first stop, Blackwaterfoot, famous for having the smallest harbour in the world (or so Craig told me), the sun was out and the place looked great. So we had a quick look and headed for a bar called the Blackwaterfoot Lodge.

The friendly lady at the door asked if she could help (this is a first for Scottish hospitality), so we said we wanted a pint and she showed us into the bar, which was lovely. We asked

Lochranza Castle, another old ruin

for our usual (pint of lager and pint of Best) only to be told that there was no draught beer as the cellar was being painted. Our suggestion that it was done when the place was shut was answered by a blank look (this is more like Scottish hospitality). It was a nice wee bar and Craig had been before and liked it, so we said we would have a wander and return in about half an hour.

Craig; *The lodge has been taken over by new owners quite recently and they are still getting the place into shape. I had actually visited the lodge two years ago and it was quite a strange experience. The décor, much of which is still the same, could be described as unique. To be honest it looks like whoever designed the bar area had an intimate knowledge of hard drugs.*

Apart from the paintings on the walls, which are quite frankly odd, the colour scheme certainly never featured in the Dulux paint chart. It reminds me of the test cards the school doctor used to check for colour blindness. Let's just say that greens and purples feature a lot.

Our visit to the pub turned to farce the moment we set foot in the place. I'm all for smartening up the decor a bit, but that

doesn't stretch to painting the cellar floor during opening hours. Besides who's ever going to see it anyway?
Given that it had been more than an hour and a half since we'd had a beer I think I did rather well not going into a giant huff. Had it been any other pub we would have made a series of very rude comments and left, forever. The thing is, the staff and the owner were so pleasant it was hard to get upset at them. I think we even apologised for leaving and promised to come back in before we caught our next bus.
John; So we had a 100 yard wander down to the 'Kinloch Bar', which is part of the 'Best Western' group and right beside the smallest harbour!
This is without doubt the worst bar I have ever been in, and I've been in a few. It was like a box with a low roof and no atmosphere at all, and the staff, of which there seemed to be plenty, just ignored you. We were cheered up on the way out by a customer who came in holding a huge pail from which he pulled the biggest sea creature I have ever seen. He said it was a lobster, but I'm sure I had heard someone earlier shouting 'release the Crakon' After checking my pants, I recovered and took a photo of it.
We were glad to be out in the sunshine for the two minutes it took us to walk back up to the Lodge.
Craig; *There was nothing else for it but to go down the hill to the Kinloch Hotel. And things certainly went down hill as far as staff and service was concerned. On the plus side they did have beer and they did sell us some.*
This hotel is very popular with the tour bus set and is rated at three stars. I'm just guessing, but I seriously doubt that it has ever won any design awards. It's hideous.
The bar itself had all the ambience and charm of a run down village hall. I would say that it would be an ideal venue for funeral teas.

The Blackwaterfoot Lodge. The pub with no beer, yet!

I had been in the place years before and wasn't impressed by the service or facilities, nothing much had changed. We drank our pints and left, quickly.

John; Craig went to the toilet and I wandered into the bar where a man was sitting enjoying a pint, so I ranted on to him about the cellar painting thing. He apologised and said it was his fault as he and his daughter owned the place. I felt bad about this so ordered the pints and changed the subject to the smallest harbour in the world' story Craig had told me. Just then Craig came back from the bog in time to hear the man telling me that was a lot of crap and that there were many smaller harbours in Arran, let alone anywhere else. Just shows you, Craig, who is much more serious than me, can talk just as much crap, at times.

The owners' daughter came up from the cellar smelling of paint and we spent a happy half hour chatting away.

The Crakon about to be released

We would have liked to stay longer, but being prisoners of the timetable, we had to leave. So we said goodbye, promised to return in the future, and headed down to a lovely seat in the sun just about 50 yards from the bus stop.

Craig; *By the time we got back up to the lodge I'm happy to say the paint had dried. In fact I'd go further. I think that we would have been far better watching that happen than go down to the Kinloch.*

Our drink in the Lodge was very enjoyable as was the conversation with the staff, and the owner/painter. At least it was after John apologised for putting his foot in it with his crack about the sanity of painting the cellar floor during licensing hours. Then it was my turn to apologise. Earlier I had exaggerated slightly by telling John that the harbour in 'Blackwaterfoot was the smallest harbour in the world. I was only kidding. Who knew he would bring it up in conversation

'The smallest harbour in the world'

with residents of the place? To say this little nugget of information came as a surprise to them is greatly understating the situation. There was a lot head scratching and a fair amount of awkward glancing around before I owned up to my little fib. It's John's fault anyway. I was only doing what he told me. He always insists that if you don't have any facts to hand you should just make some up.

John; As the bus was about due we kept a close watch on the different ways the bus could approach. We have been caught out before. Suddenly it appeared from behind the hotel and within 10 seconds had got to the stop, let a man on, and started up again. As I choked on my corned beef and mustard piece, I dived up and on to the road and flagged the bus down. Fortunately, it was not the Pole that was driving and the nice driver stopped and let us on leaving a trail of parts of pieces and other things lying about. The seagulls were swooping as the bus pulled away.

John at the bar of the Blackwaterfoot Lodge. Normal service has been resumed, at last

Craig; *We caught our next bus by the skin of our teeth. They definitely have some very strange ideas about how to run a bus company over here.*

The highlight of our journey round to Whiting Bay was the detour down to Kildonan. The scenery was fantastic and the village itself is fairly picturesque. I should have taken some photos to show John as he had entered energy saving mode just after we left Blackwaterfoot.

John; So we carried on down the beautiful west coast of Arran, past little villages with lovely names like Corriecravie, Lagg and Kildonan. I think I slept through the last one.

Our next port of call was Whiting Bay. Craig had of course, been before and asked the driver to drop us off at the pub, so the driver dropped us at the stop before the pub and we had to walk, in the glorious sunshine, about a couple of hundred yards. You would have thought the bus driver had robbed us to hear Craig.

We went into the Eden Bar and sat in the sunshine enjoying life while Craig's blood pressure got back to normal. There was a bowling green next door and after about half an hour a man and two women started to play. It was hilarious. One of them was a big fat wuman who threw the bowl about 20

The Whiting Bay artillery range

yards through the air before it hit the ground. She took bigger divots than Tiger Woods. The green ended up like the Normandy Beaches during the war. Christ knows what the green keeper would have said when he returned.

So after basking in the sun for an hour or so looking out at the Holy Isle, we wandered up to the stop to catch the next bus. I had typed out the list of times and think I made a typo, for the bus was half an hour later than it should have been, so a pint was missed and Craig's' blood pressure went back up. Auchinleck men can get upset very easily.

Craig; *The Eden Bar in Whiting Bay was a two pint stop. It was such a nice day we decided to sit outside and enjoy our beer in the sun.*

The entertainment for our short stay was provided by the antics of some strange people over the fence from us. On the bowling green a sturdily built lady was heaving the bowls around like an East German shot putter. It was hilarious. Although I would imagine the green keeper might see things rather differently.

The only annoying thing about sitting out in the sun was the attention we were attracting. Not from admiring fans I'm sorry to say but, from a swarm of wasps. They seemed especially fond of Belhaven Best.

After a slight timetabling hiccup, no blame attached to the journey planner, we boarded our bus to our next port of call. Lamlash is only four miles along the road so it was only ten minutes between watering holes. By sheer good luck we got off the bus just beside the Pier Head Tavern thereby shaving a precious few seconds off our travelling time. As the sun was still blazing down we decided to avoid chancing a bout of heatstroke and made our way inside. We were the only indoor customers. John got into a long conversation with the barman. I got into beer drinking. The lager was quite reasonable and so was the price.

John; I was relieved when the bus did eventually arrive (No. 323) and took us on another lovely run down-or is it up-to Lamlash, which I noticed is just the same as Whiting bay in some ways, but I can't think of them at the moment. So we went into 'The Pierhead Tavern' opposite The Holy Isle. For about half the length of Arran everything seems to be opposite The Holy Isle.

We decided to go inside as we were getting fed up sitting in the sun. How often do you hear that in Scotland.

It was a nice wee pub and the barman, who after 20 years in Arran still had a strong English accent. His patter was the usual barman. When we said it was a lovely day, he

The Pier Head Tavern, absolutely peerless!

answered 'he didn't know'. Although he thought he was hard done by. I've seen snails that moved quicker than him.
After a couple of enjoyable pints, we got the bus (No. 323. again) up to Brodick. By the way, there are four different bus routes in Arran, so why are the numbers all in the hundreds, do they want to sound international or something.
Craig; *Brodick was our final destination on the Isle of Arran. By the time we arrived in the town we were both ready for something to eat. Tradition dictated that we get ourselves a fish supper. I was fairly certain that Brodick had a chip shop at the pier, and for once I was right about something. The fish supper was delicious, and if anyone knows about fish suppers it's us.*
Mac's Bar on the other hand left a bit of a bad taste in the mouth. The place could do with a good steam clean, as one small part of a full scale make over. Although putting a

match to it would also improve the Brodick skyline.
In one corner of the bar there is a large, industrial looking, solid fuel stove. In another setting that could add to the atmosphere of the place. Unfortunately, in Mac's Bar it's the atmosphere that's being added to. I've never been too partial to the smell of soot. The rest of the décor was a bit on the shabby side, even without the thin coating of wood ash.
John; We arrived in Brodick at the back of five and as the weather was still glorious, had fish suppers, sat out on the prom and enjoyed them thoroughly. After the customary photograph of Goat Fell, Arran's big hill, it was across the road and into Mac's Bar, which was a really weird bar-a cross between an American country and western bar and an island retreat. Doubt if you have any idea what I'm talking about. Mind you, we had had ten pints by then. It was also a bit rough for a bar on the front of Arran's main resort. But we fitted in well.
A couple of pints later it was back on the Ferry. This time we sat outside at the back and enjoyed the scenery for about twenty minutes or so before the call of the bar was too much for Craig, so we went down and had one.
Craig; *The weather stayed fine for our ferry trip back to Ardrossan. We sat up top for the first part of the crossing but then John detected a slight drop in temperature, so we adjourned to the bar once more. You can never be too careful with changes in the weather, especially when you are travelling with someone old enough to qualify for a concessionary travel card.*
The last part of our day out followed the traditional pattern. A wee sleep on the train, big sleep for John, and a couple of celebratory drinks in the Horse Shoe Bar.
It had been a long day and , as it turned out, a very expensive one. We had been on the road, more or less, from

7.15am till 11.00pm and had spent a small fortune. But it had been worth every penny. Yet another great day out.

John; As usual we both slept through most of the journey back to Glasgow, where we decided that as it would be near closing time by the time we got back to East Kilbride, we would do our usual and nick into The Horseshoe Bar for a couple of nightcaps. They were great.

Kate, the luckiest women in the world, and my wife, text'd me to say she would pick us up at East Kilbride station. She probably thought it was the only way she would get me home.

So it was home, feeling reasonably sober, funnily enough, and to bed after another wonderful trip.

Trips financial details;

Bus fares	Zero
Train fares	£10 approx
Ferry fares	£10 approx
Food	£6 (fish supper)
Drink	£38 (approx) I'm not proud
Total	**£64 (cheap way round my arse**

The Larkhall Blues

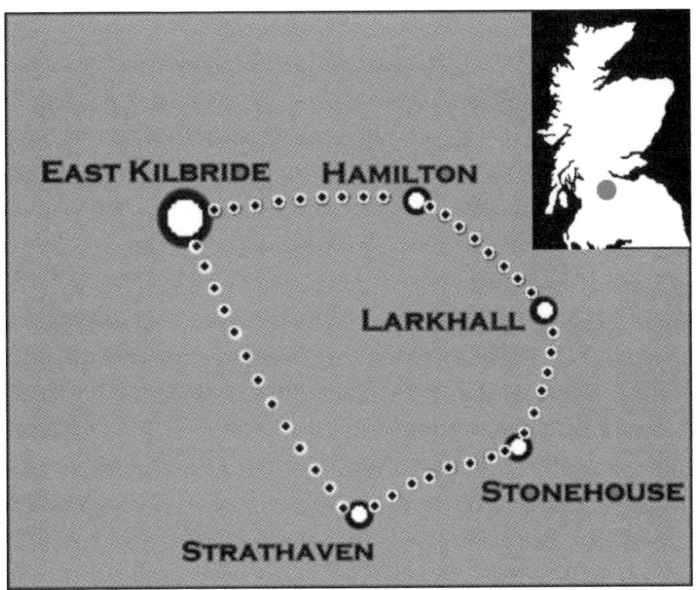

East Kilbride-Strathaven-Stonehouse
Larkhall-Hamilton-East Kilbride
(Five Buses)

John; As anybody with a knowledge of Lanarkshire geography will know this was a local trip involving only buses, so we planned to make this our cheapest ever trip, no trains or ferries-only pints to worry, or not worry about.

My worry was that we had at least an hour (or two pints) in the four places we intended to visit with only 15 minutes travel between each. That equals eight pints plus what we drink on our return to East Kilbride. The reason for my worry was that I'd promised to meet Kate at the Kings Theatre in Glasgow after she'd seen The Calendar Girls and

knew she would know exactly how many pints I'd had from 30 yards- and so it turned out.
So Craig and I wandered down to the Bus Station in plenty time to catch the 11.00am number 13 to Strathaven run by Henderson Travel (Irene's second name-amazing).
Being the East Kilbride bus station you expect to come into contact with some weird people, old and young. The first was a young jakey who thought the bus was leaving without him, although it had just arrived and the driver had told him he had to go round the bus station again for some reason or other. The jakey, who was obviously a druggie roared and shouted as much as he could with only one nostril, but when the bus came back he was nowhere to be seen. Probably forgot why he wanted the bus in the first place and just went into a trance, thank god.
While the bus was going back round the bus station an old guy came up to us and entertained us by telling things like 'his mother had been dead fourteen and a half years, the parking in Strathaven is a nightmare and he was going to drop in and see his sister-in-law in her shop in Strathaven'. He was only stopped by the arrival of the bus. We made sure he got on first so we could get as far from him as possible. Mind you, I felt terrible that I could not remember how long my mother was dead, and it's only a few years.
When the bus left we were amazed (well as amazed as you can get at our age) when the bus went a completely different way from what we imagined it would. It went to places on its way out of East Kilbride I had never seen before. It was magic, especially for someone as easily pleased as me.
Craig; *Trip number thirteen could have been an unlucky one. It certainly had It's moments. Little did we know when we set out from East Kilbride that we were about to be plagued by a lack of the most important element to any of*

our journeys. Pubs. Luckily for us we are adaptable.
Everything started well enough. We got to the bus station in plenty of time for our bus to Strathaven. We were standing waiting for the driver to make up his mind which stance his bus should be in when we made our first new friend of the day. He was very talkative and seemed intent on giving us his life story. It wasn't a great story. I had to try very hard not to look over at John while our 50 something pal wittered on about his exciting life looking after his old mother. Between snatches of this biography I suggested to John that it might be a good idea if he switched off his nutter magnet.
I suppose it was quite sad really that the poor guy was so stuck for someone to talk to that he chose us. He fairly rambled on without much of a pause for breath. Apparently his mother had died fourteen and a half years ago after a short illness. I wasn't convinced. Either she topped herself to get away from the most boring person in Scotland or, she wasn't dead at all. Maybe she faked her own death and is

Trouble looms at the Weavers

now living elsewhere under a false identity.
We made a big show of letting him onto the bus in front of us. He seemed grateful. We were grateful too. Now that we knew where he would be sitting, we knew where we wouldn't be.
John; Eventually (28 minutes later) we arrived in the nice wee square in Strathaven. The sun was shining and we were looking forward to our first pint of the day. The first pub we approached was shut. It was called 'The Weavers', so smart arse Craig instantly said 'if it's no to be The Weavers, where would we be'? I said up the road at The Bucks Head. Older readers will recognise the words to an old Scottish song. Craig and I were going to be on fire today.
I had noticed a pub up the road called the 'Bucks Head', so we wandered up and went in. Not for the first time, we were first in and the smell of bleach was noticeable, as usual. It was a reasonably nice pub, if not slightly big inside. One of these places where you could eat, drink and be merry, just don't break anything. Leaving there we headed for the 'Star Inn' which I have passed in the car many times on our way to visit our pals in Larkhall, so in we went. This was a nice wee pub with great atmosphere and an ideal pub for men of our age to go into in the morning, read the paper and pick horses (I'll have the big brown one).
Craig; *As the bus turned into Strathaven's village square we spied our first targeted pub of the day. The Weavers looked like a nice place to start our day out. It was exactly as I had imagined it, a traditional old and sturdy nineteenth century building tastefully painted. One fly in the ointment however was the fact that it was closed. Not a great start really. We quickly evaluated the situation and made a bee-line for the pub just up the road. The Buck's Head Hotel turned out to be a rather good second choice. It was quite a bit bigger than*

we thought from the outside. Having said that, we were the only customers in the place so maybe it just looked huge.
Even though we were getting the first pints through the taps that morning it was still a really good drop of beer. The barmaid was friendly and seemed to enjoy our light and witty banter. Personally I suspect that she was just being very professional.
Just when I was beginning to think the Buck's Head would be a nice place to spend a quiet night I discovered a serious drawback. They apparently run an on going talent contest, along the lines of the X-Factor. An absolute nightmare in my book. I imagine talent will be in pretty short supply in Strathaven.
We finished our beer and moved on to the Star Inn. What a contrast. The Star Inn, was much smaller than our first pub. In fact the bar was about the size of a large wardrobe. However it was a great wee pub, for men of a certain age.. That would be men of a certain age who weren't concerned about modern styling, comfort or dust free surfaces. In short, us. Actually I'm not that sure it was all that dusty but, it looked so down at heel that it deserved to be dusty. The woodwork, and there was a fair amount of it, was well worn, suggesting that not a lot had changed in the bar for many years. The beer, I'm happy to say, was in very good condition.
John; As it was approaching 12.30pm, the time for our next bus which was the 354, Stonehouse Coaches, which was to take us to Stonehouse, we drank up and said our goodbyes to the local and barman. I used to drink now and again in Stonehouse as my pal, big John lived there. So we got off the bus after only nine minutes to find that the pub (the Buckshead) was shut.

As you could see almost all of Stonehouse from where we stood and it was obvious there was no other pubs, I was a bit worried.
After wandering up and down the main, and only, street we noticed a wee deli type place that had a Tennent's pump on the bar, although it wasn't a bar, more of a wee cheap

The Buck's Head has little competition

restaurant. The big guy behind the bar gave us two pints and told us to sit at a table. He was frightening looking, so we did what we were told. He did tell us that there was a pub called the 'Cross Keys', just across the road, but we doubted it as we had walked along the main street and didn't see any pubs. However we definitely didn't want to disagree with this evil monster so we had our pints and read the menu. The pints were ok, by the way.
We wandered back out into the sunshine and Craig insisted I ask a local where the 'Cross Keys' was. So, with three pints of Dutch courage inside me I went up to these two guys sitting at the bus stop and asked them, in my toughest Govan accent where this pub was. He pointed across the road and said, just round the corner, in a Stonehouse accent. I thought

he was taking the piss, but right enough the pub was just round the corner. So we dived in and had a proper pint in a real bar. It was nice, but won't get much passing trade.

Craig; *The journey from Strathaven to Stonehouse only took about ten minutes and I remember thinking that this could be a bit of a mixed blessing. By only spending a short time travelling between pubs John was in the happy position of never being more than ten minutes away from a toilet. If you'll pardon the pun, that's always a great relief to him. The big problem was that we had very little opportunity to sober up on the bus trip between destinations. Usually much of the effects of our guzzling has a chance to wear off between towns, leaving us with the capacity to last an entire day on the sauce.*

As it turned out Stonehouse itself had a sobering effect on us. We walked the length, and breadth, of the town without finding a single pub. John was beginning to panic, after all it had been his idea to come to this ghost town. The whole town looked as if it was early closing day.

At first the only thing we found open was the bookies. Not a lot of good to us. However we did notice one of it's punters going into a café next door, so we looked in. It turned out to be a kebab shop. A licensed kebab shop. It would do if all else failed. It did. We kept on walking and searching but had to admit defeat and return to the shop. It was a scary place with a scary owner so we didn't stay long. Before we left however we heard a rumour that there was an actual pub somewhere in the town.

The Cross Keys was a large pub which makes it all the stranger that it was so hard to find. Perhaps the good people of Stonehouse don't like outsiders. The big guy in the kebab shop certainly doesn't, though I don't think he likes the locals much either. But going to the length of hiding their

A quick pint in a fast food joint

one and only pub is stooping pretty low. A good pint of lager went some way to calming us down.

John; So we wandered back out and got a bus (the 354 again) to Larkhall. Our friends live there so I know the place reasonably well. Craig had never been there and only knew about it from all the stories about them burning Catholics for fun and all the shop fronts and pailings being painted blue and white. I'm not sure about the burning Catholics story, but the rest is true.

So to add to the reputation, I took him into a pub my pal Big John drinks in called 'The Music Room', although the only music you'll every hear is flute music. Nothing wrong with that I hear you say. The walls of the pub are covered with photos of Rangers teams, players and jerseys. Craig was amazed and took some photos so people could believe him when he told them about the place. I think he liked it cause we had a couple of pints and a chat with the two barmaids who both knew my pal Big John, who goes in there every week at the same time with his pal Kirk, who used play for Motherwell.

Stonehouse's best kept secret

We left the Music Room and wandered in the sunshine down the main street, leaning slightly forward so we looked like Orangemen. I think we fitted in well, remembering that 'we are old and we are beautiful'.

Craig; *Most people living in the West of Scotland have heard of Larkhall. It has become a bit of a legend in certain circles, a bit of a no go area in others. This was my first visit. I have to admit that I have imagined what this place would be like long before we decided to visit it.*

Legend has it that there was no green man displayed at the Pedestrian Crossing as only orange men get to walk in the town. I was quite disappointed to find the place looked completely normal. That was before we entered our first pub, The Music Room.

Everywhere you look; blue paint.. The walls were covered in football related photos and framed shirts. Obviously all of that was dedicated to present day and former players of Glasgow Rangers. There was actually no real evidence that the pub's, or for that matter, the town's, favourite team ever played against any other team. The name of the pub got me wondering as to what kind of music its' patrons liked to listen to. I resisted the urge to check out the juke box. Laughing out loud might have got me into trouble, big trouble.

I didn't check every bottle and can behind the bar, but John assures me that there are no green ones.

Some might say that this is going just a bit too far to show dedication to the team. Personally, I just think it must be a nightmare for the manager when ordering stock. Although I would imagine there never was much of a demand for Appletise in Larkhall. Our next pub, the Commercial Bar was quite different from the Music Room. For a start it had barely any decoration at all. It was what I would describe as the ultimate in Scottish public house design. There are absolutely no distractions to slow down the dedicated binge drinker. We weren't slow either.

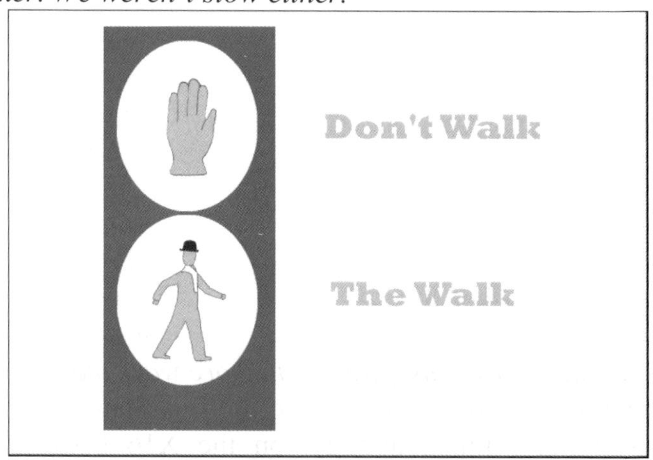

New design for pedestrian crossings in Larkhall

John; The journey took only 10 minutes or so and we were soon in Hamilton. We wandered up and into 'The Victoria

Suitably dressed for the Music Room (for those of you watching in black and white, Craig is wearing a fetching Blue shirt)

Bar', where I have been before with my pal Allan. It is a great wee pub and we had an enjoyable pint. Because of the small amount of time between pubs and the fact that this was our eighth pint, our conversation in this pub, and the next, 'The Butterburn', are a bit of a blur, but they were both great pubs and we enjoyed ourselves. Hamilton has a lot of good old men's pubs which are great places to pass an hour or so.

Craig; *Twenty minutes later we were back on the road. We visited two pubs in Hamilton but both of them turned out to be on the quiet side and just a little bit boring. I think Larkhall had wasted us, possibly in more ways than one.*

John; We made our way down to the Bus Station, with sun still shining, I think, and got on the X16 back to East Kilbride, a journey of only 15 minutes, so we arrived back in EK after being on five buses for a total of less than one hour. We were pretty pissed. We only managed one more pint in

'Hudson's', before getting fish suppers and eating them walking up the road and home.
This was about 7.30pm or so and my problem was that I had to appear reasonably sober at about 10.00pm to meet Kate, the wife, and help her home from Glasgow. By the time I got into Glasgow and walked up to the Kings' theatre, I thought I was reasonably sober, but on finding out that it was about 40 minutes before the show finished, I should have gone and had a coffee, but had two pints instead and met Kate pretty pissed, so she ended getting me home in one piece. But I had a great day in the land of the Proddy.
Craig; *Back in East Kilbride we decided to visit Hudson's, which is handily located at the bus station. It's not the most comfortable place to enjoy a quiet pint but the beer is good and reasonably priced.*
We decided to restrict ourselves to a single drink as John had a previous engagement. He had this crazy notion that if we didn't over do it in Hudson's he could appear sober by ten o'clock, just in time to escort his lady wife home from Glasgow. Even on a good day he is unlikely to appear sober at that hour. On a major excursion day like the one we had just finished he had not a snowball's.
On our way up the road I decided that, since I didn't need to be anywhere anytime soon I would visit my local to round off the day. By way of explanation, Irene was away on holiday, so 'this mouse was going to play'.
I managed just one pint before I realised that my balance was a wee bit impaired. Luckily I was still just about sober enough to realise that this condition was unlikely to be helped by scoffing down anymore booze.
As I zigzagged my way along the road I met John coming the other way. By my reckoning that meant he had managed

a good thirty five minutes sobering up time. The man was doomed.
I more or less remember getting home and I'm fairly certain I made it under my own steam. What I am certain of is that once again we had both enjoyed a great day travelling on our cheap way round.

Spends;

Bus Fares	Zero
Food	£3.50 (small fish supper)
Drink	£26.00 (about 8 pints, I think)
Total	**£29.50**

Now on Sale

(The journey continues)

They are back on the road again!

This time around the bus pass pioneers travel the length and breadth of the country. From Aberdeen in the North East down to Newton Stewart in the South West, from Dumfries to Inverness nobody is safe from their caustic commentary.
In this new book the authors set out to apply a common standard by which different pubs and hotels can be compared.
Using the 'Russell Standard', named after their favourite barman, John and Craig grade the many, many pubs they come across on their journeys around Scotland.
As you can imagine quite a few hostelries fail to meet their exacting standards.

Still Goin'

'... and there's more than a hint of Still Game about it as the feisty OAPs let rip about the highlights – and lowlights – of their travels.'
Govan Press

'... a book of their adventures has reached No 2 in the best sellers list.'
The Sun

'It's a simple idea for a book, but a clever one...
They don't pull their punches when it comes to describing some pubs in all their grotty glory.'
The Glasgow Evening Times

'Two intrepid pensioners are continuing to share their hilarious tales from trips around Scotland.'
The East Kilbride News

'...a book which takes the reader on a highly enjoyable, and very sociable, tour of the country. It almost makes you wonder why no one thought of it before.'
The Buteman